D0940038

JAMES J. O'DONNELL

SONS
OF VALOR,
PARENTS
OF FAITH

WESTBOW
PRESS®
A DIVISION OF THOMAS NELSON
& ZONDERVAN

WestBow Press books may be ordered through booksellers or by contacting:

WestBow Press
A Division of Thomas Nelson & Zondervan
1663 Liberty Drive
Bloomington, IN 47403
www.westbowpress.com
1 (866) 928-1240

ISBN: 978-1-9736-0461-7 (sc)
ISBN: 978-1-9736-0462-4 (hc)
ISBN: 978-1-9736-0460-0 (e)

Library of Congress Control Number: 2017915830

Print information available on the last page.

WestBow Press rev. date: 10/19/2017

To parents everywhere

ACKNOWLEDGMENTS

Sons of Valor, Parents of Faith would never have been a reality without the help of many people. I would like to first acknowledge all the family members who shared their sons' life stories with me. Their sons' lives were filled with many achievements and successes—both with the FDNY and in their personal lives. They all died as they had chosen to live: as men of valor. Sharing their sons' stories stirred a bevy of emotions for all the parents in this book. Their honesty and candor found within these pages bears witness to their love and admiration for their sons. Through their generous contributions, their stories will hopefully continue to add recognition for their sons.

I would also like to acknowledge Gerry Moriarty, CSW, a counselor with the FDNY's counseling services unit. Prior to earning his degrees, Gerry was a firefighter and a lieutenant with the FDNY. Gerry worked for nearly twenty years in some of the busiest firehouses in Brooklyn, and he has been cited for his bravery on numerous occasions during his career. Before joining FDNY, Gerry was an ironworker. Ironically, he worked on the construction of the World Trade Center.

Gerry was instrumental in creating the parents' group for the Counseling Unit, which sought to help the parents of firefighters killed on 9/11. Recognizing the immediate need for such a group, he selflessly addressed the concerns of the parents. All the parents interviewed cite the patience, love, and genuine concern that Gerry offered them as a significant contribution to the healing process. His compassion and understanding has helped countless firefighters deal with the tragic events of 9/11, myself included. Gerry truly has influenced a countless number of lives, and I thank him for his help with this book.

INTRODUCTION

On the morning of September 11, 2001, our world changed forever—not only in this country, but in every other country as well. There is undoubtedly no other single event occurring in our nation's history that can compare with the impact felt that day. Adding to the severity of the attacks was that it was on American soil, and it largely singled out innocent civilians. Through the use of modern media, those horrible images were transmitted live to viewers around the world.

As the world watched those burning towers, they witnessed thousands and thousands of people fleeing the inferno. They also watched several hundred firefighters, police officers, and EMTs heading into that conflagration. Sadly, when the day was over, the grim reality came to the forefront. Hundreds of those dedicated professionals had made the supreme sacrifice while trying to rescue victims who were trapped in those burning buildings. Who were these people who ran into that place when everyone else was running away?

Today, we live in a world where the word hero is bandied about and misused far too often. That is a woeful commentary on our society, and sadly for some, heroic feats seem to only occur in competitive sports. Perhaps to better understand the word, one needs only to look at the deeds performed by those men and women who perished that day while saving others to fully understand bravery. The brave men and women who made the supreme sacrifice that September morning were not only heroes—they were, in fact, men and women of valor. Their actions were motivated by a genuine altruistic concern for mankind and a true dedication to their duty. Their courage and daring can serve as an example for others to embrace and emulate.

The following pages examine the lives of nine New York City firefighters, and one New York City Police Detective who made the supreme sacrifice that day. After reading their stories, one will have a far greater appreciation for who they were and what they did. These ten men are quite different in many ways, yet they are quite similar in other ways. Their genuine concern for their fellow humans is their single most common thread.

This book will also examine the impact this tragedy had on their parents. Many of these parents were never able to claim the remains of their sons. For the parents of those firefighters who were recovered; they too endured the fear that their sons' might not be recovered. For some parents, this was not the first child they had lost. Others would lose two sons that day. One mother would lose both her firefighter husband and her firefighter son as a result of this attack.

In this text, the parents share the impact this event had on them, and it goes on to examine their subsequent spiritual and emotional journeys. All the parents in this book decided to memorialize their sons' lives in a positive way. Their goal is to see that their sons' bravery and sacrifice will never be forgotten. It is hoped that this book will help preserve their memories.

1

"I have no ambition in this world but one, and that is to be a firefighter. The position may, in the eyes of some, appear to be a lowly one, but we who know the work which the firefighter has to do believe that his is a noble calling. There is an adage which says that, "Nothing can be destroyed except by fire." We strive to preserve from destruction the wealth of the world which is the product of the industry of men, necessary for the comfort of both the rich and the poor. We are defenders from fires of the art which has beautified the world, the product of the genius of men and the means of refinement of mankind. But, above all; our proudest endeavor is to save lives of men-the work of God Himself. Under the impulse of such thoughts, the nobility of the occupation thrills us and stimulates us to deeds of daring, even at the supreme sacrifice. Such considerations may not strike the average mind, but they are sufficient to fill to the limit our ambition in life and to make us serve the general purpose of human society."
—Edward F. Croker, FDNY Chief of Department 1899–1911

***

I was working the night tour of September 10, 2001, and I was also scheduled to work the day tour on the eleventh (our night tours are from 6:00 p.m. to 9:00 a.m., and the day tours are from

9:00 a.m. to 6:00 p.m.). That evening was a fairly routine tour. We responded to about ten calls: a few rubbish fires, car accidents, and a gas leak or two. At seven thirty on the morning of the eleventh, we were called to respond as the first due Ladder Company to a reported kitchen fire. The fire was reported to be on the second floor of a fireproof building in a city-owned building project development, a short distance from the firehouse. We arrived a short time later and were confronted by a small kitchen fire, which was easily extinguished in a few minutes. One of the members of my unit sustained a minor injury, which would require me to make a few phone notifications and complete some necessary reports upon our return to quarters.

By the time we returned to the firehouse, it was nearing the change of tours. All the incoming members had arrived. I gathered the necessary report forms and headed to the kitchen to make my phone calls. The kitchen in every firehouse is the hub of all activity, and it is always the busiest and loudest at the change of tours. That morning's change of tours was no exception.

As I started to gather the information for the forms, the FDNY dispatcher announced that a second alarm had been transmitted for the World Trade Center. The dispatcher's announcement included information that an aircraft had crashed into one of the towers. I thought it had to be a small plane with a very inexperienced pilot at the controls. Commercial airline traffic into and out of the New York City metropolitan area is a daily nonstop operation. I knew of only one occasion where a larger aircraft struck a building; a military aircraft had flown into the Empire State Building on a foggy night nearly sixty years earlier.

Although there was a television set on in the kitchen, I never glanced at it as I was enjoying that first cup of firehouse coffee and scanning the reports. Soon after the dispatcher had announced the second alarm, it was followed by a call for a third alarm. The dispatchers began to call many of the department's special units and resources, which were all being directed to respond to the World Trade Center. His announcement caused me to momentarily look up from my paperwork, and as I did, I glanced at the television. The normally raucous kitchen was now quiet and soon became filled with a somber pall.

Looking at the images on the television, I quickly realized that my initial perception was anything but right. Within a few minutes of the dispatcher's notice of a third alarm, our unit was assigned to respond to the World Trade Center. We were instructed to respond along with several other companies to the entranceway of the Queens-Midtown Tunnel, which is a short distance from our firehouse. Once there, we would form a convoy with all the other units who were also assigned to respond to the tunnel, and then we were to respond to the fire.

As I boarded the apparatus, I looked at the firefighters who were assigned to alert oncoming traffic in the street outside our quarters. Looking at them cautioning the motorists was a scene I had witnessed countless times. However, as I peered further at them, I began to notice a haze of smoke surrounding them. That wouldn't have been noteworthy if the World Trade Center had been located nearby. What caused me to find it strange was the fact that our firehouse was eight and a half miles away from the World Trade Center. That was just one of the many peculiarities I would witness that day and in the ensuing months after September 11, 2001. I had never witnessed anything like it in my career with the New York City Fire Department.

As our apparatus edged out of our quarters, my nostrils soon began to sense the smoke that had circled around the firefighters in the street. We left quarters, and within a matter of minutes, we were racing toward the Queens-Midtown Tunnel. Silhouetted in the distance was the World Trade Center, and the smoke rising from the North Tower was unlike anything I had known before.

As we made our approach to the tunnel, a second plane suddenly came into view. It turned toward the buildings and then violently slammed into the South Tower. At that instant,

I closed my eyes and said a silent prayer for the people in those buildings. I came to the frightening conclusion that it was not an accident. I also came to the realization that our unit—along with the entire department and all its resources—would be stretched to its limits.

Thinking back to that haunting morning, I vividly remember how beautiful the bright azure cloudless sky looked. The temperature gave no indication that summer was waning, and a warm gentle breeze could be felt in the air. The splendor that the day had offered was an astonishing contrast to what was transpiring in Lower Manhattan that sunny September morning. At that moment in time, none of us imagined the impact this event would bring to bear upon us—and our families. No one could have imagined the number of fatalities that this act of terror would bring or the suffering it would bring to bear on the families of those who perished. The vastness of the horror it produced immediately resonated across the nation and the world. We all instinctively realized that it would be a day no one would ever forget.

The fire service is a very unique profession. To firefighters, it is never thought of as a job. For those engaged in the fire service, it is more of a calling or a vocation. Going to work is never a chore; it is something firefighters truly look forward to. Those we work with are not thought of as coworkers. They are family, a distinct family, which is not found in most other workplaces. Our own families at home are also melded into the dynamics of this unique family. In every firehouse, there is always a bevy of social activities among the members, and those activities always include the firefighters' families. The social events are aimed at creating and fostering friendships among the families. Relationships that will last a lifetime are forged.

Being a firefighter is an extremely fulfilling and rewarding experience. Day in and day out, we are called to a perfect stranger's house on what very well might be that person's worst day ever. Being able to alleviate or remedy an out-of-control situation of epic proportions for a stranger is a satisfying experience that few other careers offer. Firefighters, by nature, are a humble and modest group who shy away from the spotlight. Even after saving a life while putting their own in grave danger, the standard reply from a firefighter is always unassuming: "I was just doing my job."

A fundamental methodology consistent with good firefighting tactics is that of teamwork. To someone unfamiliar with firefighting, witnessing firefighters operate at a fire might appear to be a haphazard operation. It is, in fact, a well-orchestrated and synchronized process that demands a coordinated approach by all members on the scene. There is always a chief officer on the scene that is overseeing and directing the operations, and his perceptions are vital for firefighter safety and the rapid extinguishment of the fire. Through the use of this teamwork technique coupled with a methodical tactical scheme, firefighters are able to quickly and safely extinguish the fire. Each member of the team has a unique and vital role to play in the successful completion of the mission.

Although firefighting is a rewarding career, it is also filled with distressing and sad events that can never be erased from one's memory. For thirty years with the New York City Fire Department, I had a front-row seat to more suffering and misery than I care to remember. I have witnessed horrific death and suffering in all forms. I have seen abuse and neglect that no human should ever suffer. I have looked into the eyes of the city's poorest children who have just lost their homes to fires. Gazing at those children as they walked away with all that was left of their worldly possessions crammed into a few bags made it difficult to imagine a normal childhood for them. Their fate seemed doomed as they slowly made their way toward a Red Cross van that would transport them to a welfare hotel. I have seen, on countless occasions, people lose their homes and their entire contents. Far too often, those contents represented a lifetime of memories and could never be replaced.

I have spent my entire career with the New York City Fire Department, working in the city's poorest neighborhoods. I am honored to have served in those poorer communities; they are filled with hardworking, honest people who only want better futures for their families. Unfortunately these poorer communities always have a disproportionate rate of fire incidents compared to the more affluent neighborhoods of the city. Sadly, during my time working in those areas, I witnessed far too many innocent citizens of this city killed by fires. Knowing that you did your best will never come close to easing a mother's pain for her lost child. I have also borne witness to the pain and suffering from fire-related injuries that so many of those citizens have had to endure. Hearing the screams of a severely burned person is a sound that no firefighter will ever forget.

There is another reality about firefighting, and it is simply that firefighters are not invulnerable to injuries from fires. Firefighting is a profession that is filled with countless intangibles and unknowns. Poor building construction and alterations, illegal occupancies, arson, and hazardous materials are but a few of the obstacles that firefighters are challenged with on a daily basis. They are normally required to operate under severe conditions: extreme heat, toxic environments, unfamiliar surroundings, and thick, blinding smoke. Looking at firefighting through such a prism helps one understand some of the factors leading to the extremely high rate of injuries that firefighters sustain each year.

I have seen countless numbers of firefighters injured in my career, and although it is an assumed byproduct of the business, it still remains an aspect that firefighters never become comfortable with. Sadly, many of these injuries will be disabling, and many will never return to work. Those members will carry permanent scars and pains that will trouble them for the rest of their days. Firefighting bears no prejudices. Disabling injuries befall the youngest and oldest of us. It is an extremely difficult task to walk away from this fulfilling job because of an injury, and it is also a difficult task to watch a comrade walk away from those firefighters who remain.

Firefighters are not invulnerable to losing their lives at fires, either. My thirty-year tenure with the New York City Fire Department was marked with far too many firefighter funerals. The FDNY transmits the signal 5-5-5-5 upon the line-of-duty death of a member of the force. The signal is heard in every firehouse throughout the city, and it is transmitted over the department's radio system. The initial reaction to that message by every firefighter is sadness; we all grieve about losing a family member. That signal also serves as a reminder to all firefighters of their vulnerability.

Throughout the years, the New York City Fire Department has become the preeminent firefighting agency in fire extinguishment. A good deal of that recognition can be credited to the diverse and unique infrastructure of the city, along with its lengthy and distinguished history. The FDNY has stood on the front lines of every major emergency and fire that has presented itself to this city. They have responded and operated with a tactical approach that has been developed through the knowledge gained by that very history. The department continually modifies and makes adjustment to its tactics as science and technology make advances in our daily lives. Training is a fundamental aspect of firefighting, and the FDNY has always incorporated training into its standard operating procedures. Much of the department's training materials have been formulated as a result of knowledge that was garnered through actual experiences on the fire ground.

It is a harsh reality that, within its history, the FDNY's has endured a line-of-duty death total that is more than overwhelming. Because of this, the department has formulated a procedure to be followed at the funerals of these firefighters. Sadly, it is a procedure that the members of the department are too familiar with. The FDNY Emerald Society's Pipes and Drums always lead the procession followed by a caisson carrying the remains of the deceased. Lining the street as the caisson makes its way toward the church are always thousands of firefighters standing at attention. Every firefighter who isn't on duty is in attendance, and there are always firefighters from neighboring and distant towns and cities paying their respects as well. We all grieve along with every firefighter's family. We have all lost a brother or a sister.

In the hours immediately following September 11, 2001, the signal 5-5-5-5 became a constant message heard in every firehouse in the city. That signal would be transmitted on an almost daily basis for more than a year after the event. Incorporated into that signal, the members of the department become aware of the specific details concerning the funerals for the deceased members. It also brought with it a never-ending grim reminder of the severity and depth of our loss. This notification system was the normal procedure following a line of duty death of a firefighter; however nothing about 9/11 could ever be considered normal. The sheer magnitude of this tragedy removed it from the realm of normalcy. In the aftermath of 9/11, attending funerals/memorials coupled with countless hours searching for human remains became much more typical for firefighters. Death was all around us, and everywhere we looked, there were constant and startling reminders of that fact.

The initial hours following the last tower's collapse brought the beginning of the search and rescue operations, which would eventually become a recovery operation. There were always more than two thousand firefighters engaged in those operations, and they worked twelve-hour-on twelve-hour-off shifts for a month at a time. After a month, they were relieved by another two thousand firefighters working the same hours. This process continued until May 2002. Also present on a daily basis were other off-duty members and a large number of retired FDNY members. Sadly, many of these retired men were looking for their sons who were also members of the department. The presence of these gallant gentlemen became a source of inspiration and rejuvenation for all those working in the recovery operations. They also served as a vital testament and example to our brother/sisterhood.

When the members of the department weren't searching for the remains of victims at Ground Zero, they could be found in front of the many churches of New York City and its surrounding counties. They were gathered there for the funerals or memorials of their fellow firefighters. Many firefighters had both a memorial and funeral as their remains were found later in the recovery operation. Some days, there would be six or seven of these ceremonies, making it impossible to attend all of them. The completion of these funerals/memorials would require more than a year's time.

Watching our fellow firefighters being buried on a daily basis for more than a year truly placed a serious psychological strain on the members of the department. It is a strain that will remain with every member of the FDNY forever. The long hours working at Ground Zero coupled with the massive amount of funerals took a toll on everyone. The toxic environment that encapsulated Ground Zero was slowly taking a hold on the health of every firefighter working on the site. The long-range effects would eventually add to the number of firefighters who would perish as a result of this tragedy. No one ever complained though; that isn't what firefighters do.

Parents should never bury their children; however, for the parents of the 343 lost New York City firefighters, that would be what they would have to do. September 11, 2001, changed the rules in so many ways. Many of these parents were never able to claim the remains of their sons. For the parents of those firefighters who were recovered; they too endured the fear that their sons' might not be recovered. For some parents, this was not the first child they had lost. Others would lose two sons that day. One mother would lose both her firefighter husband and her firefighter son that day.

This is those parents' story. It is told in their own words

2

Detective Joseph Vincent Vigiano

NEW YORK CITY POLICE DEPARTMENT

Did you ever know that you're my hero?
You're everything I wish I could be.
I could fly higher than an eagle,
'Cause you are the wind beneath my wings.
Did I ever tell you you're my hero?
You're everything, everything I wish I could be.
Oh, and I, I could fly higher than an eagle,
'Cause you are the wind beneath my wings,

Joseph Vigiano was the youngest son born to Jan and John Vigiano. He grew up in the suburbs of New York City in the quaint town of Deer Park, Long Island. Joseph was many things to many people: loving husband, devoted son, a dedicated and much decorated police officer to mention but a few. Being a husband and father, however, were the roles that Joe was most comfortable in, and they came rather naturally to him. His mother recalls how much he enjoyed spending his off time with his wife, Kathy, and their young family.

Joseph's childhood mirrored his brother's and many of their friends and classmates in Deer Park. He spent much of his free time in positive and constructive activities. At an early age, he became an active member of the Boy Scouts. Eventually, his enthusiasm would give rise to becoming an Eagle Scout. Joe also enjoyed playing football and lacrosse and excelled in both. Joe and his brother John were notorious pranksters who would often work in concert to plan and bring about a multitude of practical jokes. Their father recalls that they hatched pranks that were wicked in their creativity but gentle in their impact. "They never embarrassed me," said the elder Vigiano. "They were good fathers, good husbands, and good men."

During the 1970s and 1980s, there was a group of a dozen or so young men living in Deer Park who responded to a call to serve their community. Many in this group would eventually go on to become New York City police officers and firefighters in their professional lives; they became volunteer firefighters with Engine Company Number 2 of the Deer Park Fire Department on their off-duty time. Within the department, they would be known as the "Deer Park Connection." Joseph Vigiano was one of these young men who responded to his community's call. From the outset, Joe took to the fire service and steadily rose through the ranks, eventually becoming one of the department's commissioners. During his tenure with the Deer Park Fire Department, Joe developed lifelong friendships and earned the respect and admiration of all the members of the department.

As a teenager, Joe began dating a young girl from his neighborhood. This young lady's father was a New York City police officer who would have a tremendous impact on young Joe's life. Joe was instantly mesmerized by her father's accounts of the daily routines of a New York City police officer and the many challenges that he faced during the course of his work. His eagerness to learn more about being a police officer provided him with the impetus. At seventeen years old, he applied for and took the test to be a police officer. He passed and was placed near the very top of the list of candidates.

When he told his father of his desire to join the ranks of the NYPD, his father said, "You're only seventeen."

Joe responded "Aw, no big deal."

Joe would be appointed to the NYPD at the tender age of twenty. After he completed his training at the police academy, Joe was assigned to the seventy-fifth precinct in the East New York section of Brooklyn. The seven-five was one of New York City's busiest police precincts and served one of its poorest communities. Crime was an ever-present reality, and drugs were often the common denominator that fueled much of the crime epidemic. That environment presented Joe with the opportunity to put his new skills to good work. Joe embraced his job with a passion that would set him aside from most. His fellow officers and superiors all acknowledged that Joe's dedication and bravery made him an ideal role model. Joe's great sense of humor and easygoing manner endeared him to whomever he met.

While he was assigned to the seven-five, Joe would meet the love of his life. Kathy was also a police officer. Not long after Kathy and Joe met, they were married. They settled down and purchased a home in Medford on Long Island. That union would bring them three loving sons: Joseph, James, and John. Joseph went on to graduate from SUNY Maritime and has served with the United States Marine Corps. James is currently a senior at Saint John's University and wants to join the Marines after he graduates. Both of them have taken the exam for police officer with the NYPD. Recently, Joseph was appointed to the New York City Police Department, following in both his parents' footsteps. John is a high school student who has always wanted to serve with United States Marine Corps.

Joe was extroverted and enjoyed mugging for the cameras. He was also an avid lacrosse player, having picked up the sport as a boy. After he was appointed to the department, he played for the NYPD's lacrosse team. At home, he taught his two boys how to build derby cars of pine. Eventually, he was going to do the same with his youngest son, who was only six months old at the time of Joe's death.

On the Sunday before September 11, Kathy Vigiano returned home after the first game of the season in her soccer league, bruised and tired. She was prepared to make dinner, but she saw that her husband had fixed prime rib, Caesar salad, mashed potatoes, and broccoli with cheese—while watching the baby too. She says, "All this from a guy who had previously insisted that he only knew how to make spaghetti sauce."

In 1990, Joseph Vigiano was awarded the American Legion Police Post 460 medal for valor in the performance of his duties. While on patrol, Vigiano and his partner received a radio call to respond to a shots-fired incident. Once on the scene, they approached a group of men for questioning. As they neared the group, two of the men took flight. Vigiano and his partner gave chase. During that chase, one of the suspects turned and opened fire with a nine-millimeter pistol, striking both of the pursuing officers. Even though he was seriously wounded, Joe was able to return fire, wounding the perpetrator and ending the pursuit.

Joseph Vigiano would be wounded by gunfire two more times in his career. In 1992, he was promoted to detective. After several years in the seven-five, Joe requested and was granted a transfer to NYPD's elite Emergency Services Unit. He was then assigned to ESU Truck 2 in Harlem. During his tenure with Emergency Services, Joe would garner many medals and citations for numerous rescues that he performed. His record of courage and bravery serves as a shining example of his innate altruism. Joseph Vigiano's heroism under fire ranks him among the most decorated officers in the history of the New York City Police Department. During the time that he was assigned to the seventy-fifth precinct, Joseph Vigiano was awarded the Combat Cross, the Medal for Valor, and New York Shields Purple Heart.

Joe's exemplary dedication did not allow any of his heroics to go unnoticed by the department brass either. Police

Commissioner Bernard Kerik recalled that he first met Vigiano at a support group for officers wounded in the line of duty. The commissioner recalled that Vigiano said, "I was shot five times, but I love this job." At his promotion ceremony to second-grade detective, Vigiano invited the commissioner to take part in a training exercise that called for walking on the cables of the Brooklyn Bridge. The commissioner who accepted the offer had a photograph of him and Vigiano taken atop the Brooklyn Bridge. Commissioner Kerik used to keep that photograph on his office desk at 1 Police Plaza. That photo served as a constant reminder for him of the daily dedication of all the men and women in the department.

On the morning of September 11, 2001, Detective Joseph Vigiano was on duty with the Emergency Services Unit of NYPD. The Vigiano brothers would always call their father whenever they were working. On that tragic morning, right after the first plane struck the North Tower, Joe called his dad. During their brief conversation, they shared their concerns about the attack on the World Trade Center and the inherent dangers that would present themselves. Joe had told his father that his unit would be assigned to respond within minutes. The elder Vigiano advised his son to be cautious and stay safe. He ended his conversation by saying, "I love you."

Joe simply replied, "I love you too, Dad."

Tragically those would be the last words that father and son would ever speak to each other. Moments later, Detective Joseph Vigiano and his fellow members of the elite Emergency Services Unit responded to the World Trade Center. It would be Vigiano's final response. He was only thirty-four years old, and he had been with the department for more than fourteen years. He left behind a loving wife and three young sons.

FIREFIGHTER JOHN VIGIANO JR. FDNY

His heritage to his children wasn't words or
possessions, but an unspoken treasure, the
treasure of his example as a man and father.
—Will Rogers Jr.

John Vigiano was the firstborn son of Jan and John Vigiano. His mother says, "He was filled with so much sunshine that he would light up a room whenever he entered it." As a youngster in Deer Park, John played on the high school's football, hockey, and lacrosse teams. He was also active in the Boy Scouts and became an Eagle Scout. Rather than receive the Eagle Scout designation by himself, he waited for his younger brother Joe—who was two years his junior—to complete his requirements. He did this so that they could receive the recognition at the same ceremony. His enthusiasm for scouting would carry over to adulthood. He truly enjoyed teaching and sharing his scouting experiences and knowledge with the younger members of the scouting community. Even as a youngster, giving back to his community came rather easy for John.

In high school, John began working with a local landscaper. He enjoyed the work, but he was more impressed by the prospect of having a few extra dollars in his wallet. That sense of fiscal independence led the way for young John to develop an entrepreneurial outlook at an early age.

His father's face fills with an ear-to-ear grin as he recalls John saying, "I'm going to be the next Donald Trump, Dad." The elder Vigiano added that young John often said, "I am going to make a million dollars and take care of my parents for life." Around this time, John became desirous of working on Wall Street. If he was going to be the next Donald Trump, he felt that it was a good place to start.

Academics were easy for John, and when he was in high

school, he was a member of the school's honor society. At graduation, the honor students wore gold gowns, but John didn't want any part of any expression that would single him out in a crowd. Jan says her son was "always a person who shied away from any frills and that he preferred plain things." He did wear the gold gown at his graduation after some encouragement from his mother. John attended Stony Brook University on Long Island. His parents acknowledge that he was a "home boy" who didn't care to travel too far out of his element.

John would become a member of the Deer Park Volunteer Fire Department, much like many of his friends had done. John enjoyed the firehouse, the fire duty, and the other activities associated with the fire service. He would also grow to deeply cherish the many friendships that he was able to develop within the department. Those were friendships that would last his entire life. John's father was a captain with the New York City Fire Department, but the younger Vigiano was not interested in following in his dad's footsteps. He was determined to become a millionaire, and he knew that wasn't going to happen as a firefighter. He would often tease his father and say, "You can't make any money being a firefighter."

In 1984, the Vigiano family was struck with its most difficult challenge. John Vigiano Sr. was diagnosed with throat cancer. Eventually he underwent surgery and then began what would become more than a year's work at his recovery. His ultimate goal was to return to full-duty status with the FDNY. It was a rough road for him. Some days were better than others, but he accomplished what he set out to do. John returned to full-duty status with the department and retired fourteen years later in 1998.

Watching his father suffer through this ordeal was particularly difficult for young John. John began to notice other things that were occurring during his father's illness. There was always a steady flow of visitors at the Vigiano home. The vast majority of those visitors were firefighters who worked with his dad. If his father had a doctor's appointment, a firefighter would drive him there and back. Any other chores or household repairs during this period were taken care of by firefighters from his father's firehouse. There was also a constant flow of phone calls from firefighters offering their service in any capacity.

This expression of respect and love for his father soon began to resonate with the younger Vigiano. The outpouring of love and concern was something that he had never witnessed before. He was impressed with the spontaneity that the firefighters manifested in caring for his father. Suddenly, becoming the next Donald Trump didn't seem that important to him. Much like George Bailey in *It's a Wonderful Life*; John realized just how rich his father was. At that moment, John knew that he belonged with the New York City Fire Department. Money was no longer his top priority.

John Vigiano was two years older than Joe, but his brother never let him forget that he was also four inches shorter and maybe thirty pounds lighter. The banter of sibling rivalry was typical, and they were inseparable. Besides being brothers, they were best friends. John was the quieter of the two, and he spent as much time as possible with his two young daughters. He was a terrific hockey player and an ardent Rangers fan that followed his team religiously. On several occasions, John would rent out an entire rink for his family, his brother's family, and a few other friends.

John's passion for hockey would continue even after he was appointed to the fire department. After that appointment, John would skate with the FDNY's hockey team. One year, John got some firefighters from New York and New Jersey together for a hockey tournament to help out a stranger. The money raised through that tournament went to help defer hospital costs for a young woman who was severely burned during an arson fire at a dormitory at Seton Hall University in South Orange, New Jersey. John carried the same concern and empathy for others that he developed as a youngster into his adult life. His genuine concern for others coupled with his easygoing personality caused him to make friends easily.

John would meet and marry the love of his life. Maria was a local girl who the Vigiano family had known for her whole life. Maria is a schoolteacher in a school district on Long Island. Not too long after Maria and John were married, they purchased a home in West Islip. Their marriage would be blessed with two beautiful daughters. Nicolette is a sophomore at Long Island University's C. W. Post campus, and Ariana is a junior at West Islip High School on Long Island. John was a very loving and adoring father, and he cherished every moment he could spend with his wife and daughters.

John would take the test for firefighter with the New York City Fire Department and was appointed in 1997. After he graduated from probationary firefighter school, he was assigned to Ladder Company 132. Located in the Prospect Heights section of Brooklyn, Ladder 132 was one of the busiest truck companies in the FDNY. It was also a firehouse that his father had served in. "To say he was ecstatic would be a grave understatement," his mother recalls. She added that his father was John's motivation for becoming a member of the department. John would be assigned badge number 3436; this was his grandfather's badge and only the second time it was ever assigned. John's dad ironically reflects they had their sons for thirty-four and thirty-six years.

John had begun to study for the upcoming lieutenant's test. The test is a rigorous examination that is extremely competitive and requires a serious commitment to study. John had made that commitment, and he felt he was ready for the advancement. His tenure with Ladder 132 had honed his practical firefighting skills to the point that he was more than an extremely proficient firefighter. He had come of age with the department and was prepared to embrace a position of leadership, much like his father had.

Late in the afternoon on September 10, 2001, John called his father from his firehouse. John too made it a point to call his father whenever he was working. It was a ritual that neither brother deviated from. As their conversation closed, young John said, "I love you."

His dad responded, "I love you too, son."

That would sadly be the last conversation that the father and son would share with each other. Early the next morning, firefighter John Vigiano and the members of Ladder Company 132 raced toward the World Trade Center. For all the members working that morning in Ladder Company 132, it would be their final response.

John Vigiano had served with the department for more than four years, and he was only thirty-six years of age. He left behind a loving wife and two young daughters.

> This is my commandment: Love one another as I love you, No one has greater love than this, to lay down one's life for one's friends. —John 15:12–13

JAN AND JOHN VIGIANO SR.

Parents are the ultimate role models for children. Every word, movement, and action has an effect. No other person or outside force has a greater influence on a child than the parent.
—Bob Keeshan, USMC (Captain Kangaroo)

On the morning of September 11, 2001, John Vigiano Sr. was in the living room of his Deer Park home. His eyes were fixated on the television set and the horror that was unfolding for the cameras. He had just spoken to his younger son, Joseph, a NYPD detective assigned to the elite Emergency Services Unit. His unit was assigned to respond to the World Trade Center. John had advised his son to use caution and to operate as safely as possible when they arrived. He instinctively knew that it would be a rescue operation unlike any other ever attempted in the history of mankind.

John Vigiano is a quiet and unassuming man, yet he had seen far more tragedy than most people ever witness. John, a former Marine, would spend thirty-eight years with the New York City Fire Department. His entire career was spent fighting fires in the roughest neighborhoods of Brooklyn; eventually, he would rise to the rank of captain. During his tenure with the department, John would be cited for heroism twenty-eight times. He was also an extremely dedicated fire officer who was always looking for safer and better methods to be used in firefighting. As a member of the department, he was able to develop and incorporate several life-saving procedures and tactics that the department still employs in its daily operations.

John earned a BS in fire science from John Jay College. He went on to become an adjunct instructor to the NYS First Line Supervisors Training Program and the Captains Management Training Program. These two department programs assist newly appointed officers in the transition to their new rank. He has authored many articles for various magazines such as WNYF (the official magazine of the FDNY), Firehouse, and Fire Engineering. In short, John Vigiano was a legend in the department. John's lengthy list of credentials in firefighting gave proof to the fact that his initial assessment of the unfolding events on that September morning that he was watching on television were spot on.

Sitting on his couch miles away from this horrible event and watching it transpire in front of him left him feeling helpless. His entire life had been spent responding to the calls of people in danger, and now he was forced to stand on the sidelines as an observer. But what resonated even more with John was the knowledge that his two sons would be engaged in this operation.

His extensive service with the department had given him a keen insight into the many hazards and dangers that his sons—and all the first responders—would encounter during this unique operation.

It was early afternoon when Jan Vigiano returned to her Deer Park home. She left work immediately after hearing about the attacks on the World Trade Center. She was consumed with apprehension since her sons were on duty. Jan's house was filled with neighbors and friends who were offering their concerns for John and her. All of the attention and confusion made her somewhat oblivious to those around her. Her attention was directed to her husband as they found inner strength from each other.

The Vigiano's have been married for more than fifty years, and their love and respect for each other can be easily recognized as it emanates from both of them. They only needed to look at each other to know what the other was thinking. They shared many good times as a couple and a family, and they weathered many storms too. However, they both instinctively knew that this day will challenge them unlike any they had ever experienced.

Jan Vigiano is a very private person who shies away from being in the public spotlight. She is also a deeply religious woman who uses her faith as a lifeline during times of turmoil. On September 11, 2001, Jan reached out to that lifeline and asked for divine intervention for her sons. She realized that her lifeline was to be crucial to her in enduring the terrible ordeal that had been placed before her family. Throughout her life, Jan had experienced a great deal of comfort and peace through prayer. In the aftermath of September 11, 2001, Jan placed her trust in the Holy Spirit in the hope that He might look over her and protect her family in the coming days.

On the morning of September 12, 2001, a police car was outside the Vigiano's Deer Park home. Jan and John had not received any word about their boys, but the police officer was there to escort them to 1 Police Plaza. The New York City

Police Department's headquarters was located in downtown Manhattan. They were both filled with apprehension and trepidation as the squad car made its way to police headquarters. They were both hopeful that the authorities would have some decisive information for them. When they arrived at police headquarters, they were met by a bevy of police brass and chaplains. The police representatives all expressed their sympathies and immediately offered to provide them with anything they might need. Also present were the families of the other twenty-two NYPD members who were reported missing. A pall of anxiety was cast over the families present that morning. Jan quietly prayed for a miracle that would bring relief to all the families and that all their loved ones would be found safe.

On the morning of September 13, 2001, John was escorted to the site by a team of police officers. What he witnessed that day is unlike anything he had seen in his thirty-eight years with the FDNY. His initial assessment was not a positive one, and he could visualize that the chances of survival were minimal at best. When he returned to police headquarters, he continued to maintain an optimistic presence to the other families. That night, Jan and John and all the NYPD families were lodged in an uptown hotel. John Vigiano would stay at that hotel every week from Monday through Friday until the recovery operations were completed in May 2002. On the weekends, John would return home to spend time with Jan, Marie, Kathy, and his grandchildren. He followed that grueling routine until May 2002 when the recovery efforts at the site were formally concluded.

Every morning after the attacks, the Vigiano's would be escorted to 1 Police Plaza. A Catholic chaplain from the NYPD would offer a Mass for the families of the missing police officers. After Mass, Jan would retreat into a quiet alcove in the huge building and pray for a miracle. John would make his way down to the site, which was now being called Ground Zero. The devastation continued to astonish John, yet he found comfort from the dedication of all the first responders. They were diligently laboring amid massive piles of twisted steel and crushed concrete.

Both of Jan's sons were missing when John first made his way to the site. She wasn't about to see her husband become injured under any condition. Jan asked that John abstain from participating in the actual removal of any of the debris at the site. John complied with Jan's request and became a daily observer at the site, not engaging in any dangerous activities. John's daily presence there gave encouragement to the many first responders engaged in the recovery operations. At the site, John was afforded the opportunity to interact with many members of the FDNY and the NYPD. Many of the members had worked with John and Joe, and the interactions and conversations provided John with a deep insight into the amount of love and respect that his sons' coworkers had for his boys.

John was not the only retired FDNY member who had a lost an FDNY son. There was a group of active and retired firefighters whose sons were members of the department and had been declared missing at the scene. The fathers held a daily vigil throughout the operation. They actively took part in the every aspect of the search and recovery process of the operations. Having all of these FDNY fathers on the site served as a tremendous source of great inspiration for all those who were engaged in the recovery operations. The mere presence of these men provided all the recovery workers with the incentive to continue their duties no matter how fatigued they might have been.

Jan and John were overwhelmed by the amiable and professional considerations that were extended to them and all the families of the missing NYPD police officers. The Vigiano's had never had much interaction with NYPD, and they lauded all the members of that department for their care and concern for them. To this day, they are both actively included in numerous NYPD events and ceremonies that recognize the efforts of NYPD members on 9/11. John credits former Commissioner

Kerik and former Commissioner Kelly along with then-Chief of Department Joseph Esposito as being extremely considerate and helpful to them during this ordeal.

Firefighter John Vigiano's remains were never recovered from the site; however, his brother's remains were recovered. On the day Joseph was recovered, his father was present on the site. One of Joe's fellow officers was quoted in a local paper: "We searched for many days and weeks with Joe's father present every day standing by with a strength and dignity I had never witnessed before and haven't since. When we found Joe, ironically, it was not us comforting Mr. Vigiano; it was him providing a hug and words of comfort to myself and my brothers in ESU."

The Vigiano family held a memorial Mass for John and a Mass of Christian Burial for Joseph. Both these liturgies were attended by thousands of friends, family members, and members of both departments. At both services, John spoke to those in attendance and requested that everyone who had known his sons simply e-mail him with a short reflection of their relationships and interactions with his sons.

John's intent was to collate these different stories into a collection that each of their grandchildren would have of their father. Since all their grandchildren were very young on 9/11, John wanted to ensure that all the grandchildren had a special insight into the character of their fathers. John had not envisioned the enormity of the response to his proposal. John has received more than a thousand responses. He has reached out to an author who agreed to organize the e-mails and transpose them into two books. One is a blue leather-bound book with the NYPD emblem on the cover, and the other is red leather-bound book with the FDNY emblem on its cover. Each of these books offers John and Jan's grandchildren a deeper understanding of the type of men their dads were and the relationships they both had with their friends. The books are a work in progress since John continues to receive e-mails from friends of Joe and John even to this day.

A short while after her sons' funerals, Jan ran into a mother of an FDNY firefighter who was also killed on 9/11. Jan and the woman were friends prior to that fateful September morning. She told Jan that she had joined a group of other FDNY parents who had lost a son. The group was called the "Parents Group" and was under the tutelage of the FDNY's counseling services. The group had weekly meetings, and Jan quickly immersed herself in it. After speaking to her friend, Jan realized that she needed to become a member of the group. Jan was glad that she took advantage of enrolling in the group, and it was extremely beneficial to her. Jan was able to receive a great deal of comfort by sharing her feelings with other parents who were experiencing the same feelings. She is grateful for the many friends she made through the group, and she continues to maintain those friendships to this day.

In the weeks immediately after 9/11, President Bush visited New York City. One of the purposes for that visit was to meet with the families of the first responders who were killed at the World Trade Center. Jan and John had the opportunity to meet with the president, and he conveyed his sympathies to them and all the other families who were assembled. After speaking with Jan for a few moments, President Bush said, "You remind me a lot of my mother."

Jan said, "When are you going to get that guy Bin Laden?"

President Bush replied, "Now you really sound like my mother."

Just prior to September 11, 2001, Dick Wolfe executive, producer of NBC's Law and Order, was working on a pilot for a new series about the NYPD's Emergency Service Unit. One of the officers highlighted in the production was Detective Joe Vigiano. The series never came to fruition due to logistical reasons, but after 9/11, Wolfe toyed with the idea of a documentary about the Vigiano brothers. He reached out to the family and inquired about their feelings about such a project. John told the producers that he was fine with the concept, and he was interviewed throughout the film.

The documentary aired on the USA network. *Twin Towers* played to rave reviews throughout the country. On the night the film's premiere, Jan and John were guests of Laura and George Bush at the White House for a private viewing with the first couple. Jan and John recall the Bushes being brought to tears as they watched this powerful and moving story unfolding. The film's producer, Peter Jankowski, said, "We tapped into an emotional thread that's universal. I'm really proud of the fact that the family has a fitting tribute to their two sons."

Spending an evening at the White House with the first couple was something that neither Jan nor John had ever given any serious thought to—before or after September 11. It is also something that nether had aspired to at any time. The Vigiano's are a private couple, yet they are filled with pride when they reflect upon the men their sons grew to be. They are proud to share the courageous and honorable lives that their sons led with the world. Besides spending time with President George W. Bush, the Vigiano's have visited with the Joint Chiefs of Staff and many other government officials. They remain a humble couple, yet they are somewhat amazed by the people and places they have come to know in the aftermath of 9/11. "This isn't me. I am a fireman. Now, all of a sudden, I am doing things you could read about," said the elder Vigiano. "I feel when I'm called to do anything, I have to put up a good front and honor my two sons."

Jan and John are equally as proud of both their daughters-in-law. They speak lovingly and with great admiration for the efforts of these two women in raising their children. They readily acknowledge the love and care that they demonstrate on a daily basis. As a couple, the Vigiano's make every effort to spend as much time with their grandchildren as possible. They enjoy sharing stories about their fathers with the children, and they take great pride in helping them appreciate what good men their fathers were. Recently, John's grandson James accompanied him on a trip to Guantanamo Bay Naval Base in Cuba. The purpose of their visit was to bear witness on a firsthand basis of how our government addresses terrorism and terrorists through the legal system.

John continues to make it a priority and visits as many Wounded Warriors as he can. Several times a year, he makes his way to the Walter Reed Hospital in Washington DC, sometimes accompanied by his two grandsons, to visit wounded soldiers returning from Iraq and Afghanistan. "We have a common bond. If September 11 had not happened, they may not be in these beds. Because they are, I am here to say thank you." As a former Marine, John readily acknowledges the connection between the sacrifices that his sons made and the sacrifices that these heroes made and continue to make.

John also serves our veterans by serving as a member of the Honorary Council of the Hope for the Warriors Foundation. In memory of his sons, John graciously volunteers his time and resources to help Gold Star families and wounded heroes. He became close friends with actor Gary Sinise while visiting the troops in Iraq. John actively advocates for the several scholarship awards that are presented yearly in honor of the Vigiano brothers.

John continues to give back to firefighters around the world. He is able to call on his thirty-eight years of experience and share that vast expertise with other firefighters in a positive manner. John remains a frequent guest speaker at numerous firefighting seminars held around the country throughout the year. He also continues to share his vast knowledge of firefighting with those active firefighters by authoring numerous technical guidebooks and procedural manuals. He has collaborated with other professional firefighters to develop successful training practices for today's firefighters. John firmly believes that proper training

SONS OF VALOR, PARENTS OF FAITH

methods are an essential tool in reducing firefighter injuries and deaths.

On the loss of his sons, John Sr. reflects, "I don't have any could'ves, should'ves, or would'ves. I wouldn't have changed anything. It's not many people that the last words they said to their son or daughter was "I love you." Those three little words are very meaningful, but when they are put in John Vigiano's perspective, they take on an even deeper and much more powerful message.

The pain of losing their sons will never go away for Jan and John. Jan says, "Birthdays are extremely difficult times to deal with—along with other milestones in the boys' lives." When you look at Jan and John, their love for each other becomes clear to any observer. When they speak, their faith in God is manifested. No words or sentiments could ever ease their grief; it is obvious that their love for each other and their love of God are two resources that they share on their journeys.

Every September 11, the Vigiano's honor their sons in the same way. They begin with Mass and then go to a nearby diner for breakfast. After breakfast, they drive to the cemetery where their sons are buried. They bring folding chairs and spend the entire day in prayer, reflection, and remembrance. They are amazed at the amount of visitors who come to honor their sons while they are at the cemetery that day. Those visitors continue to serve as a reminder for Jan and John of just how many lives John and Joe touched in such a positive manner.

The Vigiano's are active in the many scholarship funds that are raised to honor their sons. They are advocates for all the families who were murdered on that tragic September morning. They continue to share their fathers' life histories with their grandchildren. They are firmly resolved to share their sons' stories with the world. They want the world to know that their sons were men of honor and courage whose last acts were saving humankind.

3

Lieutenant Kevin Donnelly FDNY

*Courage is the first of human qualities because it
is the quality which guarantees the others.*
Aristotle

Kevin Donnelly was born on July 7, 1958, in Rockville Center, New York. He was the second of four children born to Cecilia and Edward Donnelly. Donnelly grew up in Levittown and attended his parish's elementary school, Saint Bernard's. He and his two brothers, Edward and Brian, graduated from Pope Pius X Catholic High School in Uniondale. His sister, Mary, would go on to graduate from Holy Trinity High School. Catholic education was an important subject in the Donnelly household, and Cecilia and Ed took the necessary steps to ensure that all their children received faith-centered educations. Ed was a postal worker, and Cecilia was a school crossing guard. Resources were limited, but Ed was always able to earn some extra income by working numerous odd jobs over the years that provided the funds for parochial educations for their children.

As a youngster, Kevin loved to run and swim. Those were also his favorite activities as an adult. From an early age, KD—as he would come to be known—developed an entrepreneurial approach toward life. By the time he was twelve, he had established a successful and thriving lawn care business. He would continue to operate his business right up to the day of his death. Kevin was able to hire his friends and classmates, ensuring that they too would receive paychecks. Kevin also worked as a lifeguard at the town's pool; working there gave him a free pass to one of his favorite pastimes. His innate business savvy would later enable him to become a successful real estate investor after he joined the fire department. All the while, Kevin knew what he wanted to do with the rest of his life: become a member of the New York City Fire Department. The only obstacle in his path was his age, and he patiently waited until he had reached the minimum age of appointment: twenty-one.

All of us have our own personal quirks that help define us. Kevin's personal quirk was that time didn't really matter to him. He was often late for appointments, dinner dates, and family functions, but he was never late when it came to the FDNY. Sometimes he would be driving when the urge would hit to go swimming in the ocean. When it came to interacting with his lawn care customers, he was always curious about how their lives were going. He took the time to engage each of his customers in a meaningful dialogue. KD made a special effort to look in on his widow clients to see if they needed groceries or assistance with chores. Kevin would also bring this caring and engaging approach toward life to the fire department. It didn't matter if you were the richest or poorest person, he was never judgmental. He had always shown nothing but compassion for those he met.

Kevin earned degrees from SUNY Farmingdale and Nassau Community College. KD supported himself with his lawn business and working in the heating and air-conditioning field. On July 8, 1979, the day after his twenty-first birthday, Kevin Donnelly was appointed to the New York City Fire Department. Kevin wouldn't allow the fire department to interfere with his educational goals. After his appointment, he would enroll at Hofstra University and receive a BA in business. Not satisfied with a BA, Kevin studied fire science at John Jay College, and he went on to receive a master's degree from that institution. Armed with his new degree, Kevin joined the faculty of New Jersey City University as an adjunct professor. The flexible work schedule that firefighters enjoy allowed him the free time to teach several fire science courses on days he wasn't working in the firehouse.

KD led an extremely active life, and it was hard to keep up with his hectic schedule. In between working at the firehouse and attending classes, Kevin would spend his downtime swimming or running. As a youngster, he swam with the Levittown Swimming Association. His love of running would provide him with the impetus to complete the highly competitive New York City Marathon three times. Kevin and several of his friends were involved in a study group for the promotional examination for captain scheduled for October 2001. The promotional examinations are offered every four years and are always extremely competitive. Kevin and his friends began a grueling study regiment many months before the examination was scheduled to be administered. They would attend classes together and exchange information at weekly study group meetings.

Kevin became a member of the Wantagh Volunteer Fire Department while he was awaiting his appointment to the FDNY. He had followed his older brother Ed's lead by joining that department. KD's father cites this period in Kevin's life as the time when he truly began to know what he really wanted to do with himself. Kevin totally immersed himself in the Wantagh Fire Department, seeking to learn as much as he could. That enthusiasm for the fire service would remain with Kevin Donnelly his entire life.

When Kevin was originally appointed to the FDNY, he was assigned to Engine Company 222, the "Triple Deuce" in the Bedford-Stuyvesant neighborhood of Brooklyn. He later transferred to Ladder Company 176, the "Tin House" in the

Brownsville section of Brooklyn. Eventually Kevin was promoted to lieutenant and assigned to Ladder Company 3 in Manhattan. Kevin Donnelly and the FDNY was a match made in heaven, each of them complementing one another. He had found his true calling with the fire department. The job offered him a satisfying and rewarding experience that was unlike anything he had ever been exposed to. KD had matured into an ideal firefighter and fire officer, and he was looked up to and admired by his coworkers and his chief officers.

Over the course of his career with the fire department, Kevin showed keen insights into the technical aspects of firefighting. His degree in fire science helped him grasp the complex principles of firefighting. His personal experiences had given him mastery in the practical application of those principles of firefighting. Kevin Donnelly was a modest man who would never boast about anything. His record as a firefighter and fire officer indicates that he was someone to be admired. During his tenure with the New York City Fire Department, Donnelly operated with or directed units that attained six unit citations. In addition, he was the recipient of four medals for acts of heroism and bravery.

Those are some extremely impressive numbers for a firefighter to amass over a twenty-two year career with FDNY. KD was modest and reluctant to talk about those rescues. In fact, he made it a point not to wear the ribbons awarded from those citations on his dress uniform. Kevin Donnelly was able to touch upon the lives of so many people—and he was the instrument that saved their lives—but he chose to not talk about it. There are many New Yorkers who are alive today simply because of the bravery and dedication to duty of Kevin Donnelly. His humility was a character trait that his fellow firefighters admired greatly. Those firefighters would say that Kevin always let his actions speak louder than his words.

The title of lieutenant brings added responsibilities. When Kevin was promoted to lieutenant, he took those added responsibilities very seriously. One critical component of his role as an officer was to ensure that all the members under him were proficient in all phases of firefighting. Kevin could always be found with the firefighters in his firehouse studying new techniques and reviewing the standard procedures and tactics used by the department. Kevin was able to share his wealth of knowledge and his vast personal experiences with the younger firefighters in his firehouse. That information helped his company perform at a high level of excellence, and it helped perfect the individual skills of every firefighter assigned to that company.

The night before September 11, 2001, Kevin telephoned his sister in Florida to see how she was doing. A viral infection in 1993 had left Mary in a wheelchair, and Kevin was always concerned about her. She told him about a pool lift she thought could give her more independence. "I told him it cost $2,002— and I had the $2," she said. Within the week, she'd received a check for $2,000 plus a two-dollar bill for her son, James. Kevin never lost sight of the strings that held his family together.

At 9:00 a.m. on September 11, 2001, Donnelly was relieved from duty after working the previous twenty-four hours. However, the first hijacked plane hit the North Tower of the World Trade Center while the FDNY was changing shifts. Kevin and the other members of the FDNY who were off duty realized the gravity of the event and knew there were many people who would be in need of help. Ladder 3 had already been called to respond to the World Trade Center. Kevin and the off-duty members of the company quickly gathered their firefighting clothing, commandeered a few taxicabs, and began to make their way toward the site.

Official reports indicate that Kevin had climbed up to the sixtieth floor of the North Tower before heading back down the stairs. His ability to reach such a height is a testament to his physical conditioning and stamina. He started to make his way down right after the South Tower collapsed. Those reports show that Kevin was able to make it all the way down to the fifteenth floor before stopping to help more people who needed to be rescued. Kevin's last conversation was with a firefighter from Ladder Company 5. "Hey Lou, we've got orders to get out!"

Kevin replied, "Go ahead. I'll catch up as soon as I finish helping these women."

Lieutenant Kevin Donnelly and eleven other firefighters from Ladder 3 would never make it out.

A memorial service was held for Kevin Donnelly on October 6, 2001, at Saint Francis de Chantal in Wantagh, New York. His body was eventually found on Tuesday, March 12, 2002, and he was buried at the Holy Rood Cemetery in Westbury on Monday, March 18, with a lone fire department piper playing "Amazing Grace" in the distance. Ironically, Kevin was buried the day after Saint Patrick's Day, his favorite holiday. Over the course of his twenty-two-year career, Donnelly's bravery and courage brought credit to the New York City Fire Department. His dedication serves as an example for all its members.

CECILIA AND EDWARD DONNELLY

Amen, I say to you, if you have faith the size of a mustard seed, you will say to this mountain, 'Move from here to there,' and it will move. Nothing will be impossible for you."
Matthew 17:20

When Ed and Cecilia Donnelly received the news that Kevin was one of the firefighters unaccounted for; they were devastated. Ed and Cecilia have been married for more than sixty-two years, and nothing has been as difficult as wrestling with the loss of their son. Soon after they received the news, they joined the FDNY's parents' group. Ed and Cecilia became regular attendees at the Thursday night meetings at the Freeport firehouse.

They both credit this group as a powerful tool in their personal healing process.

Sharing their feelings with the other parents was a truly moving and uplifting experience. Participating in group events with the other parents was beneficial to their healing. Whether it was a prayer or reflection by a parent or simply releasing balloons, those events resonated as positive measures. At a meeting, the mother of a firefighter told Ed to think of his son every time he finds a coin. It is something that he continues to do. Sharing their feelings with the group was a very positive experience for Cecilia and Ed.

One significant difference that Ed and Cecilia had from most of the other parents was age. Another significant difference was that Kevin was older than most of the other sons. He had been with the department for more than twenty-two years. Despite those differences, the Donnelly's felt very comfortable with all the other members of the parents' group. Cecilia and Ed's perspectives also provided the parents' group with a broader viewpoint that everyone could benefit from. The common bond they shared with the group far outshone any differences that might have existed.

Cecilia and Ed both share a deep faith that they say was instilled in them when they were children. They credit their parents with imbuing them with their values and work ethics. Listening to Ed speak is like watching the History Channel unfolding in front of your eyes. Ed grew up in Brooklyn and remembers the day his parents lost their home in the Depression. He approached his father and asked for his permission to enlist in the service at seventeen. His father refused and told him to wait a year. Ed's father had served in the trenches of France during the First World War. He knew firsthand the horrors of war and was in no hurry to send the youngest Donnelly brother off to war. Ed's older brothers were a United States Marine on Iwo Jima, and a crew member in the Army Air Corps serving on a bomber flying missions over Europe. When Ed's eighteenth birthday came around, the war was over. Ed found out that he had a perforated ear drum, which would have prevented him from serving.

Having lived through the Depression, Cecilia and Ed know the consequences of poverty and its effect on families. Throughout their lives, they have strived to provide the very best for their children. The Donnelly's appreciate the things they have, and they thank God every day for what they have been blessed with. They strongly believe that the key that unlocks poverty is education. Every one of the Donnelly children graduated from college and then went on to earn a master's degree, as well. Cecilia and Ed share the belief that a life without faith is a life that is lost. They shared their gift of deep faith with their children.

They know, in their hearts, that their beloved Kevin is in a far better place. When they refer to him, they simply say, "He has been called home." Their faith is fervent, and they are at peace knowing that their son is with God. As I listened to them speak, I recalled a passage from the Trappist monk and mystic Thomas Merton: "You do not need to know precisely what is happening, or exactly where it is all going. What you need is to recognize the possibilities and challenges offered by the present moment, and to embrace them with courage, faith, and hope." Cecilia and Ed embrace the challenges in their lives with courage, faith, and hope.

The Donnelly's daughter Mary, recently lost her husband having succumbed to a heart attack. Mary lives in Florida, and the distance makes comforting her difficult for Ed and Cecilia. The other Donnelly children are spread out across the country, and Ed and Cecilia miss them dearly. They visit with them and look forward to spending time with them and their grandchildren. They wish they could see them more often, and Cecilia and Ed pray for their family members daily.

It was an extremely difficult time for Cecilia before Kevin's remains were recovered. However, she began to experience some inner peace and tranquility after he was found. Cecilia feels remorse for all the parents who were unable to recover the remains of their children. She continues to remember those parents in her daily prayers, hoping that their grief may be somewhat eased. Their belief in Catholicism was able to sustain them throughout their ordeal.

Cecilia and Ed remain filled with pride over the accomplishments that Kevin was able to achieve in his short time with us. They have a profound respect for what all firefighters do on a daily basis, and they are pleased that Kevin was able to fulfill his lifelong dream of being a New York City firefighter. They find comfort in knowing the significant role Kevin played in rescuing so many people during his service with the department. They are grateful for the care and concern shown by the FDNY's Counseling Service Unit. They acknowledge and appreciate all their fellow parents who they shared grief with.

They miss their son dearly and share some regrets that he was taken far too early. Ed knew that Kevin would have become a great father someday. They also are confident that Kevin would have risen higher through the ranks with the department. Kevin's sharp intellect and attention to detail would have ensured high marks on future promotional examinations. Cecilia is sure that Kevin would have continued teaching fire science and sharing his knowledge and experiences with others. The New Jersey City University has a scholarship named in Kevin's honor, and it is something that Ed and Cecilia take a great deal of pride in. The scholarship recognizes Kevin as a member of the New York City Fire Department and a faculty member.

More than thirteen years have passed since that horrific September morning. Cecilia and Ed admit that their age precludes them from being more physically active. They acknowledge that they don't do as much as they once did, but they accept it as another step on their personal journeys. They continue to be active in their parish and share the liturgy with their fellow congregants. They remain very insightful and stay abreast of world events through both print and electronic media. They have witnessed many changes in the world. As they think back on those changes, they say, "Some of those changes were for the better, while some weren't."

They are troubled by recent current events, but they remain prayerful and hope for a lasting peace. Amid all the disturbing news throughout the world, they remain resolute in their faith. They know that they will someday be called home to be blessed with eternal life and be reunited with their beloved Kevin.

4

Firefighter Michael Mullan FDNY

*Even if it's a little thing, do something for those who have
need of a man's help something for which you get no pay
but the privilege of doing it. For, remember, you don't live
in a world all your own. Your brothers are here too.*
—Albert Schweitzer

When I asked Theresa Mullan to describe her son, she replied, "I remember asking him what he wanted to be when he grew up." She shared his responses:

Age five: "A motorman on a big train."

Age ten: "A catcher on the New York Yankees like Thurman Munson."

Age fifteen: "I want to play the piano like Jerry Lee Lewis and get all the girls."

Michael Mullan was the middle child born to Theresa and Patrick Mullan. Michael was a premature birth, and his first few weeks were critical. Theresa's pregnancy with Michael was complicated further due to the Rh factor and the problems that often arise in the delivery of a baby. As an infant, Michael fought to overcome what seemed to be overwhelming odds and thrived. It was a trait that would remain with Michael throughout his life.

Whatever the challenge, Michael would rise to meet it head-on—and always with his ever-present grin on his face.

Michael grew up on Jordan Street in the Bayside area of Queens. It is community of small semi-attached homes and streets lined with trees; it is also a neighborhood where everyone knows one another. It's a community filled mostly with police officers, firefighters, and other blue-collar workers. Scattered throughout the area, there are many churches and synagogues. All the houses of worship play major roles in the family lives of the residents. The Mullan family was no exception to that norm. Their parish was an immense focal point in their lives.

Michael spent his grammar school years at Blessed Sacrament School. Blessed Sacrament is a parochial school that is part of the Mullan's' parish. Michael's days were filled with CYO basketball, bowling, and swimming. He was a Boy Scout and an altar server, and he took music lessons. His neighborhood was filled with children his age, and he made friends with many of them.

Michael was spontaneous during his early school years, and his behavior would often place him in front of the principal. That was always followed by a phone call to the Mullan household. The message was terse: "Mrs. Mullan, you must come and see me so we can discuss Michael's behavior." Theresa was always polite in her responses to the principal. She simply said, "No, thank you. I know Michael's behavior. There is nothing you can tell me that I would disagree with or be surprised by." Michael's grammar school years were filled with antics that had his classmates in stiches, and he tested the patience of his teachers.

His antics would eventually be met with scolding, grounding, and loss of privileges. Afterward, he was always contrite and promised never to act that way again. Theresa says, "The good behavior would last about a week." Underneath the façade, there was a very different side of Michael. He shoveled the snow out of the widow's driveway. He ran errands for his elderly neighbors.

He had a paper route so he would have spending money, and he helped his sister with her Penny Saver route. After he graduated from Blessed Sacrament, he went to Holy Cross High School.

Holy Cross was a Catholic high school within walking distance of the Mullan's home. Michael's four years at Holy Cross were quite different from his grammar school years. Michael still enjoyed life, and his life continued to be filled with laughter. Theresa credits much of the difference to the brothers of the Congregation of the Holy Cross. She witnessed their ability to channel Michael's exuberant energy into many positive outlets. At Holy Cross, he joined many of the after-school activities—orchestra, jazz band, and drama—and starred in several renditions of Broadway stage productions. Michael discovered the stage and enjoyed being on it. There were no more behavioral phone calls to the Mullan home while Michael was a student at Holy Cross High School.

Holy Cross is a college preparatory school, and the courses and activities have been designed to promote spiritual, emotional, and psychological growth. Its mission statement claims that a student's education and development are reinforced by active participation in the school, the community, and places of worship. Civic and moral responsibility are exemplified and promoted. The school challenges students to be inquisitive and vigilant in searching for the truth.

During his sixteenth summer, Michael landed a summer job at a camp for children with cerebral palsy in upstate New York. The camp had a steady flow of campers. Every two weeks, a new group would arrive and replace the prior group. Each of the campers required total care: feeding, bathing, dressing, and exercise. Michael earned high marks from his supervisors at the camp, and Theresa believes that his time at the camp had a deep impact on his life.

In the spring of 1985, Michael Mullan graduated from Holy Cross. Theresa and Pat were filled with pride as he received his diploma. He had a surprise for his parents shortly after that graduation ceremony. Michael announced to his family that he had enlisted in the United States Army. Michael's dad, Pat, was a supervisor with the New York City Department of Sanitation and a reservist in the Army. His parents were initially concerned, feeling that he might have been too young to make such a commitment.

Michael said, "I've been in school all my life. I need a break."

In hindsight, Theresa acknowledges that it was an excellent decision on his part. He responded well to the discipline and learned to set goals. The well-structured lifestyle the military offered helped him remain focused on those goals and encouraged him to raise the bar at every turn. Theresa was impressed by how Michael challenged himself. His innate exploratory nature would prod him to sign up for jump school. He earned his paratrooper badge after completing his third jump. Michael was sent on to Fort Sam Houston in Texas to continue his advanced training. Upon completion of his training, he became a certified X-ray technician.

After basic training, he was given leave and returned home to visit his family. He was proud of his accomplishments and wanted to see his former teachers and show off his uniform. He headed over to Holy Cross to visit some of his former teachers. After a cordial visit with the faculty, he bid them farewell and headed home. As he was walking down a corridor, he passed the detention room. His curiosity caused him to peer into the classroom. A dozen or so depressed students were writing lengthy punishment assignments for whatever violations they had been found guilty of.

Michael was consumed with a mischievous urge. He marched into the room with a military stride and gazed at the students. In an authoritative voice, he barked, "Gentlemen, you are dismissed." Instead of the laughter he anticipated, the students gathered their belongings and almost knocked him down as they flew toward the exit. Quickly realizing the error of his ways and fearful of being caught by one of the brothers, Michael made his way to the exit as well.

When the brother in charge of detention returned to an empty room, he learned in short order that an Army soldier in uniform had dismissed everyone in the classroom. Michael had not even arrived home before the phone was ringing. The brother explained to Theresa that alumni visits were always welcomed, but alumni participation in current disciplinary matters was not sought after or appreciated. Theresa didn't know what to think. What would she tell Pat when he came home? Theresa began to laugh to the principal's dismay. She told him that he was no longer a Holy Cross student. As a United States soldier, he belonged to Uncle Sam. Perhaps he should bring up the issue with him. The brother was not very amused by her response, but it did cause Michael to become a legend at the school. It's not hard to see exactly where Michael got his great sense of humor.

While Michael was in the service, he passed the written test for firefighter with the New York City Fire Department. When Michael completed his four-year enlistment, he was honorably discharged. He followed his father's lead and enlisted in the Army reserves. Everyone who has been on the list for firefighter with FDNY knows that the process is lengthy, and Michael was no exception. While he was waiting for his list number to be reached, Michael enrolled in Queensborough Community College. He earned an associate degree in applied sciences. He passed the New York state boards, earning a license as a registered nurse.

Michael worked as a registered nurse at Saint John's Hospital's emergency room until he received his notice of appointment from the fire department. At the fire academy, his military training and experiences came to the forefront. He quickly began to master his new career. When he graduated from the fire academy, he was assigned to Ladder Company 12 on West Nineteenth Street in the Chelsea neighborhood of

Manhattan. Michael kept his part-time nursing job while with the FDNY. He joined the nursing team in the emergency room at Mercy Hospital on Long Island.

Michael had come a long way from being a spontaneous youngster at Blessed Sacrament School. He began to attend classes at Hunter College to pursue his bachelor of science in nursing. He earned a black belt in karate. He was a commissioned officer in the Army reserves and attained the rank of captain. He had found his niche in the fire department. He discovered his love of comradeship, and it was a perfect match with his enormous sense of humor. What stood out amongst his peers was his dedication to the job and his desire to be the best that he could be. Michael developed a reputation as the company prankster, often making himself the victim in his antics.

One night a young boy was admitted to the emergency room at Mercy Hospital. The boy Steven had a 104-degree fever, and Michael was assigned to care for him. An IV helped hydrate him to bring down his fever. The boy was very ill and deeply frightened. He confided in Michael that he was deathly afraid of needles.

Michael said, "If you let me insert the needle, I will take you to my firehouse, dress you up in my gear, and let you sit on the fire truck—and you can even slide down the pole."

The boy responded, "You can't be a fireman. You're a nurse."

Crossing his heart, Michael said, "I promise you, Steven. I am both."

Two weeks later—fully recovered—Steven and his mother visited the quarters of Ladder Company 12. Steven had a great time doing all the things that Michael had promised.

On the morning of September 11, 2001, Michael Mullan was on duty with Ladder Company 12. Ladder 12 would be assigned to respond to the World Trade Center that tragic morning. Upon their arrival, Ladder 12 was assigned to aid the search and evacuation of the Marriott Hotel. While searching the upper floors of the hotel, Ladder 12 heard a firefighter transmit a Mayday call on his radio. Michael responded with his officer and another firefighter to assist the trapped firefighter. Sadly, that would be the final act for all three members of Ladder Company 12.

At age thirty-four, a few weeks prior to 9/11, Theresa said, "Michael, what are you now that you are all grown up?" She cherishes his response.

"I am a New York City firefighter. I am a registered nurse. I am a captain in the United States Army Reserve. I play the piano like Jerry Lee Lewis, and I get all the girls.

THERESA MULLAN

May you live every day of your life.
Jonathan Swift

Theresa Mullan is a woman of great faith. As a young woman, she explored whether she was being called to a religious vocation. Although she concluded that she wasn't being called, her faith grew even stronger through that examination and journey. Theresa credits their belief in God as the single most compelling force that helped her and Pat struggle in the aftermath of September 11, 2001. In the darkest moments, their faith became the lynchpin that guided and reassured them.

Faith sustained them during the time Michael was listed among the missing. Nearly a month after the attacks, Pat and Theresa's prayers were answered. Michael's remains were recovered on October 7, 2001. A Mass of Christian Burial was held at Blessed Sacrament Church—the same church where Michael had served as an altar server. It was a beautiful Mass that was well attended. All of Michael's family, thousands of firefighters from around the globe, neighborhood friends, and members from his Army unit assembled to pay their respects for a neighborhood hero. Michael's sister, Kelly, has a friend who offered a beautiful operatic rendition during the ceremony. During the Mass, many of Michael's friends and coworkers shared their experiences with him to all in attendance.

Throughout the wake and after the funeral, Theresa and Pat were blessed to hear stories about their son from his co-workers, friends, and military comrades. The stories gave the Mullan's a different perspective of the type of man their son had become. The nurses told of how Michael was always the first to open his wallet for a gift when a nurse became pregnant or an illness had befallen a nurse or her family. His coworkers in the emergency room would relate stories of how he was the ideal professional. They also noted that he was filled with compassion and sensitivity for the patients he was called to serve. His fellow nurses shared countless stories of the energy and humor that he brought to the workplace every day. His commanding officer of his Army unit took note that Michael was always the first member to report for duty and the last to leave. He remarked that Michael's concern and generosity for those under his command was an inspiration to all the members of his unit.

The firefighters from his firehouse shared stories of a dedicated young man who loved life and lived life with passion. His great sense of humor and love of pranks made him a hit with all the firefighters he worked with. His devotion to the FDNY made him a firefighter who others wanted to emulate. Michael's neighborhood friends shared how Michael had thwarted a robbery of an elderly man in the area. That man shared that Michael would go back to look in on him and run errands for him. He remained good friends with the kids he grew up with and was revered as the life of the party among them.

Michael's siblings, Kelly Ann and Patrick, spoke lovingly about what it was like growing up with their brother. Music was a central component in the Mullan household, and all the children played an instrument. Sibling rivalry is normal behavior in any family, and Michael was a master at instigating many conflicts that flared up in their development. As they matured, their love and respect for each other grew. Patrick knew that he could count on his brother for anything at any time. Kelly recalled always being in dire financial straits as a college student. A letter to Michael asking for a twenty-dollar loan was always answered with a forty-dollar check.

Several months prior to September 11, Pat and Theresa purchased a home in suburban New Jersey. Pat had recently retired from his position with the sanitation department, and Theresa was about to retire from her job as a registered nurse. They kept it a secret from Michael because they were going to give their house in Bayside to him. Theresa could never see Michael leaving that house or that block. Michael was welded to the memories that the Mullan house held, and the neighborhood represented so much of what he truly was: a local boy who made it in the real world.

I never had the opportunity to meet Pat Mullan because he passed away prior to my meeting his wife. Theresa shared her thoughts on the type of man her husband was with me. Pat was a quiet and reserved man who preferred that she discipline the children. He was a loving husband, a dear friend, and a devoted father. He was a hardworking man and a devout Catholic who actively professed his faith.

After Michael's funeral, Pat and Theresa heard so many wonderful stories about the person their son had become. Pat said, "I should have been the man he was."

Theresa responded, "He could never have been the good man he was if his father wasn't such a good man."

On the morning of September 11, 2001, Michael was on duty in his firehouse. He called home and spoke with his father. The airways were filled with the graphics of the burning towers, and Pat had been watching them unfold from his living room.

Pat said, "Be careful on that truck today."

Michael told his father that they were ordered to respond to the World Trade Center. At that moment, they weren't sure where they would be assigned. He said, "Dad, I love you. Please tell Mom, Pat, and Kelly Ann that I love them too. Good-bye, Dad." It is somewhat ironic that Michael said good-bye to Pat, because he never said good-bye to anyone.

In the months after 9/11, the FDNY sent out newsletters to all the families affected by the tragedy. The letters provided information about groups that were available to help family members in dealing with their grief. One letter announced the formation of a group for parents of firefighters who were killed that day. Theresa knew she had to attend the group to find some help for her in coping with this tragedy. Pat was not so inclined to attend the meetings. He could not witness the grief of other parents or share his own. He would share his feelings with Theresa, but he spent much time in contemplation and prayer. Experts in the field agree that we all grieve in our own ways.

Theresa embraced the parents' group and the many other parents who were also suffering. She readily developed friendships with many of the other parents and remains active with them socially. In the group, she felt secure in expressing her feelings and listening to the feelings of others. She became politically active with several other parents on issues that often failed to take the views and opinions of the parents of the firefighters into consideration. She voiced her views on the construction of the memorial at Ground Zero and proposed that the feelings and sentiments of the families of those who perished be taken into consideration prior to starting any construction. She also was an advocate for the FDNY's creation of the World Trade Center Medal, which is awarded annually by the department and endowed by the parents of the 343 firefighters lost that day. The award recognizes the efforts and work of the FDNY's parents' group as well.

The Mullan family chose to honor Michael by giving back to

the places that Michael had been a part of. The family awards two scholarships at Queensborough Community College for students enrolled in the nursing program. They present an annual scholarship in Michael's name to Holy Cross High School and provide a cash award to students graduating from Blessed Sacrament School in Bayside.

The United States Army chose to honor the memory of Michael Mullan by dedicating a building at Fort Eustis, Virginia, to him. The building serves as headquarters for the Joint Task Force Civil Support and was dedicated on June 14, 2012. "He was dedicated to the job, to his mission, and to serving others," said US Air Force Major General Jonathan T. Treacy, JTF-CS commander, during the ceremony. "He was devoted to his fellow firefighters and service members, and he was driven to helping others in the truest sense of service before self."

Theresa was asked to unveil the bronze plaque on wall of the entranceway to the building, and she proudly complied.

Mullan Hall, named in honor of Michael D. Mullan, Captain, USAR. CPT Michael D. Mullan, USAR, was a decorated U.S. Army Reserve nurse, an emergency room nurse, and a New York City firefighter, cited for bravery. He died during the September 11, 2001, terrorist attack on the World Trade Center while rescuing civilians and fellow firefighters trapped inside the adjacent Marriott Hotel. As a first responder, CPT Mullan was committed to saving lives while serving his country as a Warrior Citizen. That core principle is the backbone of Joint Task Force Civil Support, whose mission was established to save lives and mitigate loss in the event of a chemical, biological, radiological or nuclear attack on the United States.

The JTF-CS lobby is adorned with display cases of Mullan's personal belongings, such as his army uniform, New York City firefighter helmet, medals and citations, and a framed collage featuring photos of Mullan on the job as a firefighter and soldier.

During the ceremony, Theresa said, "This is the closest I'll ever come to winning the lottery, and I thank you very much. Can you believe a hundred years from now, someone will say, 'I'll meet you at Mullan Hall'?"

The following are the thoughts and sentiments of Michael's brother.

My World Trembled Today

Patrick Mullan II

This poem is dedicated to New York City's bravest—the selfless men and women of the fire department of the city of New York. This poem is especially dedicated to the brave souls of Ladder 12, the pride of Chelsea. Most of all, this poem is dedicated to my brother, Michael Dermott Mullan, Badge Number 7830, who courageously gave up his life in the Marriott Hotel on September 11, 2001. His honor and glory will not be forgotten.

My world trembled today.
The slaves of evil smote us with fire and dismay!
Destruction and death, they carried on the morning breeze.
Their evil mission was to bring us all to our knees.
Ground rolled, earth groaned, and the sky went black.
Death came from the sky; our country was under attack!
Alarm bells rang out; many knew that they would die.
They dialed their cell phones to tell their loved ones goodbye.

5

Firefighter Christopher Santora FDNY

I am William Wallace! The rest of you will be spared. Go back to England, and tell them there, that Scotland's daughters and her sons are yours no more! Tell them Scotland is free!
—Braveheart

Christopher Santora grew up in the Long Island City neighborhood of Queens. Long Island City is not much different than any other residential community in New York City. It is a veritable melting pot of every ethnic and religious group imaginable. The basketball courts and the streets provide the arenas for young boys to learn sports and funnel their energy in a positive manner. Those venues are the backdrops where lifelong friendships are formed as well. Chris was no different than any of the other kids in the neighborhood. One of the best means for a young boy to get along in the neighborhood was to become active in sports. Basketball, stickball, softball, and tennis were the sports that held Chris captive. Chris's warm nature and quick wit enabled him to make a bevy of friends. Growing up in a melting pot, Chris's friends were a mirror image of his community. Who you were or what you were weren't important to Chris. If he liked you, you were his friend forever. The friends he made he made for a lifetime.

Being able to excel on the basketball courts wasn't the only requirement for making it in New York. One has to have street smarts and book smarts. Chris was blessed to have the ideal combination of these necessities. Chris's most distinguishing characteristic was his sense of humor. Chris was also born with what his dad Al called the gift of gab. He often thought that his son would have been a terrific lawyer. Chris was a natural prankster, and no one escaped from becoming a victim to one of his tricks. As the only son in the Santora home, his four sisters naturally were the primary targets for many of his pranks. His biggest desire in life at that time was to have a brother, and he would often complain about the house being filled with too much "girl stuff."

When Chris was fourteen years old, his aunt died. Kathleen was his mother's sister. Kathleen had two children. Megan was five, and Daniel was three. They came to live with the Santora's. In the Santora household, family always came first. Megan and Daniel were family. With Daniel as a member of the household, Chris finally had the brother he so desperately craved. Daniel was a good deal younger than Chris, and he was physically challenged. Daniel had been sick since birth, and his illness forced him to wear braces on his legs. Quickly after moving in, Chris and Daniel developed a special relationship. Chris always found the time to play with Daniel and entertain him. Al and Maureen remember how much Daniel looked forward to spending time with Chris—and how happy he was when they were together. The Santora's fondly recall how that special relationship helped Chris mature into a kinder and more caring young man. Sadly, Daniel would pass away shortly after his seventh birthday, leaving the Santora family heartbroken again.

Chris Santora's early years were filled with the typical activities that most young boys his age were involved with. Boy Scouts, Little League, and the YMCA were some of the organized programs that Chris loved and excelled at. Swimming, skiing, and basketball were not just pastimes. They were the things that he was most passionate about. Although he was short in stature, Chris's exceptional speed would even the playing field in any athletic competition. He was a tenacious and fierce competitor in every event that he engaged in.

Though he was blessed with a natural talent for sports, Chris Santora was an exceptional scholar as well. He had been born with the gift of a photographic memory, empowering him with the ability to read something once and recall it. His sisters would become frazzled as they labored over their homework, but Chris was able to complete his studies in short order. As soon as he completed his homework, he was off to the basketball courts. Chris's mother was a schoolteacher, and all the Santora children were instilled with an understanding and a deep respect for education. Chris was a bright student, and he wasn't the least bit shy about expressing his opinions. Chris would challenge any teacher who wasn't prepared for an assignment or lacked in subject knowledge. His opinions often created trouble for him, but he never backed down from his convictions if he felt he was right.

When it came time for Chris to attend high school, he was placed in the honors program, which only required a little more effort from him. He welcomed the challenge. The honors program afforded Chris a little freedom in his coursework and provided him with the opportunity to study subjects from different areas. Chris continued to play clarinet in the high school orchestra. He had taken it up in middle school, and it also was something he came to enjoy. He became quite proficient and continued to play after high school.

Chris could have attended the local high school, but he selected a school with a more challenging and stimulating curriculum. Travel time to this school meant a ninety-minute commute each way, but he thrived socially and academically. His high school years were also helpful in broadening his circle of friends. When it came time to pick a college, Chris initially chose Pace University and majored in accounting. It only took one semester at Pace before he decided to transfer to Queens College. Chris couldn't see himself as an accountant; he was deeply enthralled by American history. Ultimately, Chris would graduate from Queens College with a degree in history.

Armed with his new degree Chris landed a position as a substitute teacher with the New York City Board of Education. It was a job that he really enjoyed, and he felt every bit alive in the classroom. He relished the fact that he was helping young people learn about the world in which they lived. He felt comfortable connecting with his young students and sharing the life stories of the heroes in history that he grew to admire. Chris always admired those who fought against tyranny and oppression, and he soon discovered that he was a natural at sharing the experiences of his heroes with his students.

"The heroes he chose from history are the ordinary heroes, the people who made a big difference," said Maureen. "He was very impressed that an average citizen would step up to the plate and do the right thing." Reading about people such as William Wallace and Paul Revere excited Chris and fueled his desire to delve deeper into history. In the classroom, Chris's quick wit coupled with his great sense of humor made him an instant favorite among his students and won him the admiration of his fellow educators.

In 2001, Chris was offered a full-time teaching position, but he turned the offer down. He was on the list to be appointed to the New York City Fire Department and knew he was about to be called to begin his training as a firefighter. Chris didn't think it was fair to have to leave his students during the semester. Chris's deepest desire was to follow in his father's footsteps and become a member of the FDNY. He knew from his dad just how satisfying the life of a firefighter could be. The test for firefighter in the FDNY is an extremely competitive process, and higher scores on the written and physical tests improve the chances for appointment.

Chris spent more than a year both studying for the written test and conditioning for the physical component. All of his preparation paid immense dividends, and Chris achieved perfect scores on both the written and physical portions of his examination. He became a member of the first class of probationary firefighters called from his list in 2001.

After he completed his probationary firefighter training at the FDNY's fire academy, Chris was assigned to Engine Company 54. Engine 54 is located on the West Side of Manhattan adjacent to the Theater District. Engine 54 shares quarters with Ladder Company 4 and Battalion 9.

Chris Santora had worked the night tour on September 10, 2001, and was due to be relieved from duty at nine on the morning of the eleventh. That morning, Engine 54's firehouse was one of many that received the call to respond to the World Trade Center. Chris and all his comrades from Engine Company 54, Ladder Company 4, and Battalion 9 responded to that alarm that morning. Chris Santora and fourteen other brave firefighters from that firehouse raced toward those burning towers, and none of them would ever return. Chris Santora was just twenty-three years of age, and he had only graduated from his probationary training eight weeks prior to that response. Sadly, seventeen other members who had graduated in the class with Chris would also make the supreme sacrifice that fateful day.

Chris Santora had some other goals besides firefighting, and they were lofty goals as well. For the time being, he had placed them on hold. He had achieved his lifelong dream of becoming a firefighter, and he was enjoying every second of it. He had a clear vision of the many things that he wanted to achieve in his lifetime. His dad had cautioned him about the inherent risks in firefighting and how many young firefighters' careers are cut short due to serious injuries. His parents had always encouraged him to learn as much as he could and to always continue to explore the world around him.

Chris confided in his parents that he wanted to return to school in the future to pursue doctoral studies in American history. He had entertained ambitions of teaching at a university and writing a few books after he retired from the fire department. Chris Santora had made it. His whole life was now in front of him.

MAUREEN AND AL SANTORA

To one who has faith, no explanation is necessary.
To one without faith, no explanation is possible.
Thomas Aquinas

Al and Maureen Santora are a couple who share a deep love for one another, and that love quickly becomes obvious to anyone they meet. Over the course of their marriage, they have experienced many of life's joys along with some sad moments too. Their love for each other has been the vehicle that guides them through the good times and comforts them during the bad times. They have so much in common in their values and their desires. Their strongest common bond is their faith. Their faith is central to their existence, and it is through that faith that the Santora's can better understand the world in which they live. Maureen and Al are devout Catholics, and they firmly believe that their faith is a gift from God. As parents, they lovingly share this gift of faith with their children.

Firefighting is a career path that requires a genuine sense of service and caring for humankind. Chris Santora didn't have to look very far to find role models for that type of dedication to the community. Maureen Santora is a retired New York City Board of Education teacher with a lifelong record of service to the children of New York City. Over the years, Maureen has had a positive impact on hundreds of children.

Maureen authored two books for younger children and one for middle school-aged children. *My Son Christopher* is the story of a mother's unconditional love for her son. "No matter what he ever did, I loved him because he was my son," Maureen explains. The book teaches children that every hero, like Christopher, leaves behind a mom, a dad, brothers, and sisters they were very special to. Christopher's story reminds the reader of the importance of a person's life and how that person can inspire us to achieve greatness. The book tells the story of her beloved son and the challenges he faced when he was growing up.

Her other children's book is titled *The Day the Towers Fell*. This is a rich and straightforward description of what happened that terrible day, and it offers an appropriate description of those events for younger children. Maureen's years as an early-childhood educator and staff developer clearly come to the forefront. This book offers caring and practical guidance for parents and educators to help children understand the importance of kindness and the effects of hatred. Two of Maureen's daughters, Patricia and Megan, collaborated with her on the two projects. They were able to skillfully provide special illustrations that were suitable for younger audiences.

Maureen's third book is, *We Remember*, and is intended for middle school-aged children. This book is a heartwarming collection of personal stories that were written by friends and family members of those people who were killed on 9/11. Their message is a simple one that reminds us that life is sometimes short—but we are all loved by someone.

In honor of their son—among the youngest of the 343 firefighters who gave their lives saving others at the World Trade Center—Maureen and Al Santora have founded the Christopher Santora Educational Scholarship Fund to make a difference in the lives of other children. Promoting education is a cause that is very dear to the Santora family. All the proceeds from the sale of Maureen's books are used to help sustain the fund.

How does one cope with such a devastating loss? Maureen credits her faith in God and her assurance that He would never present her with a challenge that He didn't also equip her to face. Secondly, Maureen and Al decided to advocate in honor of a son who had always been outspoken and opinionated. Many consider grief a private matter, but Maureen has learned the healing power of keeping the memory of her beloved son alive.

Al Santora is a retired member of the New York City Fire Department, having risen through the ranks to become a deputy chief. Al had spent more than thirty-five years with the department. In a career that spanned that much time, Al Santora has seen far more tragedy than the average person. Al has also seen and been involved in a significant amount of rescues, fires, and emergencies. Participating in a rescue, a fire, or an emergency is the greatest reward any firefighter can receive. Deputy Chief Al Santora retired with an envious legacy: he was a "good guy." In fire department language, that is short for a giant among giants and someone to be looked up to and admired.

Al weathered the war years within the department. On a typical night tour, a company would respond to twenty-five calls and often encounter three or four substantial fires. It wasn't the least bit uncommon that beer bottles were hurled at responding fire trucks. Filled metal garbage cans were tossed off rooftops at firefighters who were actively engaged in extinguishing fires. Violence and anger were omnipresent every day, and the FDNY was always in the crosshairs. Arson for profit was a daily occurrence. Many firefighters were killed, and many others became seriously injured during fires that were directly attributed to this nefarious behavior. Unfortunately, not many of those events ever reached the newspapers. They became so common that their value lost any newsworthiness.

Sociologists and economists offered an array of explanations for why New York City was burning during the sixties and seventies. They also have an assortment of reasons for the crack epidemic that plagued New York City in the eighties. The widespread use of crack cocaine presented the fire department with a new broad range of responses due to the effects of the drug on many communities. The explanations and reasons suggested by sociologists and economists didn't matter much to Al. He just got back on the truck and put out the fires or went on to the next overdose.

Amid all this chaos, it's reasonable to assume that some people could have become angry and bitter. Al's character wouldn't allow him to fall victim to those emotions. Al held a different perspective. He knew he was helping and caring for others. No one had ever called Al Santora judgmental. More importantly, Al always felt like he was doing the job that he loved and that he had signed on to do to the best of his abilities. As a firefighter and a father, Al felt that this was a perfect job for Christopher—and he was anxious to see that desire come to fruition. Al envisioned Chris becoming an officer and making his way through the ranks very much like he did.

Al began studying for promotional examinations during this social revolution. He was an extremely knowledgeable firefighter, and he became quite proficient at taking his promotional examinations. Each promotion brought new responsibilities, and he embraced them all, rising to the challenges that they presented. All the firefighters and fire officers who worked alongside and under him agree that Al always passed on his knowledge and skills concerning firefighting to everyone. His paramount concern was always the safety of his members, and he was instrumental in continuing the rich traditions of the New York City Fire Department.

Al Santora's proudest moment in his fire department career was when he witnessed his son's graduation from probationary training at the fire academy. Al was forced to retire just prior to Christopher's appointment to the department. He had sustained a serious injury at a fire, and it precluded him from remaining with the department. He has reservations that he wasn't active in the department when Chris was appointed, but his joy at Chris's success far overshadowed any of those misgivings.

September 11, 2001, presented itself to New York City as a bright sunny day. It was the first day of school for the public school system. Parents and children were busy scampering about and familiarizing themselves to a new time schedule. The summer had passed. It was supposed to be a significant and memorable morning for Maureen Santora too. That bright September Tuesday was Maureen Santora's first day of retirement, and she was ecstatic to grab a few more minutes of sleep rather than having to rush off to work. As she slept peacefully, she had no idea how unforgettable that day would be.

Suddenly, she stirred from her deep slumber.

"Wake up, Maureen! A plane has gone into one of the Twin Towers," Al shouted. The Santora's eleventh-floor high-rise apartment afforded them a bird's eye view of the Manhattan skyline, and they raced toward the window. They were overcome with shock at what they saw. Thick black smoke was emanating from the North Tower. They silently shared their bewilderment about how it could have happened. After watching that horrific sight for several minutes, Al and Maureen noticed a second plane in the vicinity of the Twin Towers. The plane circled the South Tower, and within a matter of seconds, the plane hit it. They came to the realization that what they were witnessing was not an accident. Their thoughts were filled with confusion and fear.

A short time after the second plane hit, the South Tower collapses. Al and Maureen both looked on in disbelief as the tower disappeared from view. Throughout Al Santora's years of service to the FDNY, he had seen structural failure in buildings. He knew instantly that the survival rate for those occupants would be minuscule. Sadly, Al's observations were correct. Al and Maureen's apartment, which had presented them with such an enviable view of the New York skyline, had given them an unobstructed view of the carnage. Regrettably there were 2,753 innocent individuals murdered on that bright September morning at what was once the World Trade Center.

While those events were transpiring, they realized that Chris is still at work. They tried to reach him, but they were unable to. Al concluded that Engine 54 has been assigned to respond to the Trade Center. He decided that he was not going to remain at home and wait for a phone call. He made his way down to the site. Once he arrived, he was in a state of total disbelief. He was dumbfounded by the amount of devastation. Al searched for Engine 54, but he was unable to locate them. None of the firefighters at the scene could help. Looking over the devastation, Al realized that the search and rescue operations in the coming weeks would stretch the resources of the department to the limit.

Al had arrived at the scene without any firefighting clothes. He was able to find some firefighting clothing for himself from the numerous trucks at the scene. He quickly sized up that there was a shortage in the command structure and offered his services to the fire chiefs who were operating at the scene. In conjunction with the chiefs, he started to assist in directing some fire companies' operations. He also aided in coordinating relief for the other companies that had been working for longer periods. It didn't take Al long to understand that there was a significant breakdown in communications among the units who were operating at the scene. No one was positive which companies were missing, and no one had any idea how many firefighters were unaccounted for. The sixteen acres that the Twin Towers once proudly rose above had been reduced to a mountainous pile of smoldering steel. As Al surveyed the site for Engine 54's apparatus, he realizes that countless pieces of department apparatuses were buried under tons of debris. The scene on the ground was unlike any other operation that Al had ever witnessed.

Later that night, Al returned home for a shower and a change of clothes. Early the next morning, he arrived at 1 Police Plaza. He desperately searched for any information concerning the whereabouts of Chris and his company. After spending some time there, he was unable to produce any positive leads. New York had been dealt a blow like no other blow before.

In the early stages of the disaster, confusion was commonplace. It would take some time to reestablish an orderly chain of command and restore some order to the city. Al decided to revisit the site, but he was unable to gather any information about Chris and his company. He was not the only FDNY father—active or retired—who was searching for a son. Dozens of active and retired firefighters were doing exactly what Al was doing. They were all experiencing the same anguish and frustration. Al was physically and mentally exhausted, but somehow he made his way back to Long Island City to comfort Maureen.

Over the next few days, Maureen and Al were in constant contact with Chris's firehouse. They began to get some information, but it was not that promising. Through the members of Chris's firehouse, they learned that all fifteen members who were on duty that morning were unaccounted for. Although Christopher was relatively new to his company, the families of the other missing firefighters quickly embraced the Santora's into their fold. It was a hectic period for all of the families of the missing firefighters. The days turned to weeks, and the weeks turned to months—and they still didn't know the fates of their loved ones.

A multitude of firefighters, police officers, EMS workers, and construction workers painstakingly sifted through thousands of tons of twisted steel and crushed concrete in a desperate search for survivors. Those workers would labor twenty-four hours a day as they went over the site with a fine-toothed comb in search of survivors. A constant smoldering of materials from beneath the surface lingered with all who labored there long after they left the site. As time went on, the operation would become a recovery operation. The search and recovery operations were unlike any other in the history of humankind, lasting nearly nine months.

The Santora's were in the unenviable position of having to bide their time while they prayed for a miracle. Maureen was frantic and didn't know where to turn. She even visited fortunetellers, anxiously hoping for the slightest ray of light. She was convinced that her beloved Christopher was somehow still alive. When she was not praying, she was calling hospitals and morgues. The waiting and absence of information were slowly crushing her.

Al was beside himself. He was hurt and angry. He didn't know what he could do to make the situation any better. He realized that he was not in the right frame of mind. He needed to talk to someone. Al reached out to the fire department's counseling unit and was referred to a peer group. The group was made up of active and retired firefighters with sons who were unaccounted for. Al was able to gain some comfort from the group, and they shared their common grief. They wrestled with their grief and frustration and supported each other.

Al is proud of the good work that the fire department counseling unit has done with all the families and members affected by the events of September 11. He clearly understands that it was virtually impossible for anyone to have anticipated a tragedy as immense as this. He appreciates how the counseling services unit hit the ground running and was extremely proactive in its approach to helping all its members and their families.

In the weeks after the attacks, the numerous cruise line companies that were based in New York made some of their cruise ships available to the families of those who were lost. The ships would pick up family members in Brooklyn and steam to the North Cove Marina, which was adjacent to the World Trade Center. The family members were escorted to a private viewing area to observe the daily activities that were taking place. Family members were not permitted to venture beyond the viewing area. All that was required of the family members was to make contact with the cruise line and set up a scheduled time for a visit.

Al and Maureen were regular participants in the program and attended every two weeks. In the weeks after 9/11, pedestrian and vehicle traffic was on limited basis in Lower Manhattan. Special identification passes were required for anyone attempting to access the area, and special security checkpoints controlled all movement throughout the area. Having the ships available for the families of victims proved to be an excellent method of providing them with direct access to the site.

Maureen orchestrated a special memorial ceremony in conjunction with the cruise line to honor Chris, and his classmates from probationary firefighter school. Maureen had selected All Soul's Day for this ceremony since that feast day held a great deal of significance for her and Al. Maureen arranged for several priests, rabbis, and ministers—along with more than two hundred friends—to participate in the service. Once they arrived at the viewing area, they assembled for a multi-faith prayer service. After the prayer service, eighteen firefighters from Chris's probationary firefighter class proceeded to the bottom of the pit. Each of the firefighters held a lit memorial candle and placed it in the pit; each candle was representative of one of their classmates who perished that day. No one spoke to one another for a week after it.

As the weeks turned into months, the hopes of finding Christopher seemed slimmer. Maureen remained steadfast that he would be recovered. Sadly, only one member from Chris's firehouse was ever recovered. Jose Guadalupe of Engine Company 54 was laid to rest on October 1, 2001. The Santora's attended the funeral and the memorial services for all the other firefighters from Chris's firehouse. By Thanksgiving, all the members of Chris's firehouse had memorial services except for Chris Santora. Maureen was still praying for a miracle.

Al and Maureen finally made the decision to have a memorial Mass for Chris. It was a heart-wrenching choice, and it was the hardest thing that Al and Maureen had ever done. Al firmly believed that it was the first step in the healing process and hoped that it would help them both. Over the next few days, Al made sure all the arrangements were taken care of. Al struggled with the difficult task, but he knew it needed to be done. A father shouldn't be burying his son, and it troubled him deeply. Christopher's memorial Mass was scheduled for December 1, 2001, at Saint Rita's Roman Catholic Church in Long Island City.

Bishop Ignatius Catanello from the Diocese of Brooklyn would celebrate the Mass along with the pastor and curates from Saint Rita's. The fire department made sure Chris received full honors, and the FDNY Emerald Society Bagpipe Band played a salute in his memory. Chris's old high school's concert band offered several musical selections. The school's glee club also offered a presentation. More than a dozen friends and relatives offered eulogies, each sharing a part of a special relationship with Chris. Because of his young age, it was the first death that many of Chris's friends encountered. They were greatly troubled by their young friend's death. For some friends, it was their first funeral.

On November 28, 2001, Maureen Santora headed to a Manhattan hotel to attend a luncheon sponsored by the United Federation of Teachers. Maureen and several other recent retirees were recognized for their distinguished service and dedication to education. With Chris's memorial Mass only three days away, she was reluctant to attend. Al insisted that she go. Midway through the luncheon, Maureen noticed someone standing in the wings. She recognized the lieutenant who was assigned to Chris's firehouse. When she approached him, he informed her that she should return home with him. A department car was waiting for her.

In the vehicle, she noticed a chief and a driver. As the car raced over the Queensboro Bridge toward Long Island City, no one told her anything. Her mind was filled with an eerie apprehension that something was terribly wrong with Al. The car stopped in front of her building.

In her apartment, she was overwhelmed by the amount of strangers. Several staff chiefs from the fire department, the chief of department, a fire department chaplain, a few deputy commissioners from city agencies, and a representative from the chief medical examiner's office were sitting with Al. She was immediately relieved to see Al, and he appeared to be perfectly fine. He assured her that nothing was wrong with him, but he cautioned her to brace herself for what she was about to hear.

The medical examiner apologized for the error they had committed. Christopher's body had been recovered, but because of procedural errors, he was mistakenly identified as Jose Guadalupe. Those remains had been interned nearly two months prior under the premise that it was in fact Jose Guadalupe's remains. The Santora's had been in attendance at Jose Guadalupe's funeral.

Maureen was not sure about anything. She was elated to have Chris back, yet she was somewhat disturbed by the revelation. Al and Maureen agreed that the medical examiner ensured that appropriate measures had been taken once their error was detected, and they acknowledged his honesty. After Maureen had a few minutes to absorb the medical examiner's message, the room was filled with a deafening silence.

How could that possibly have happened? The medical examiner's office admitted that it had mistakenly identified Christopher as one of his fallen comrades. Both men worked at Engine Company 54, and the identification process was based on x-rays that pathologists felt matched a rare congenital formation on two vertebrae in Guadalupe's neck. Unbeknown to them and to the firefighters' families, Christopher Santora shared the same rare condition—and the body was actually his. The medical examiner stated that it was a very unusual situation where two people who worked together had exactly the same congenital anomaly. Al Santora said he was told the odds were one in five million for two people to share this neck anomaly—and one in five trillion that they also would work together.

Maureen Santora was in a state of shock. She excused herself and went to her bedroom to regain her composure. She told Al that she had to speak with Jose's mother. She was overjoyed that her prayers had been answered and she had Christopher home again. Maureen was deeply troubled for Jose Guadalupe's mother, and she could only imagine how painful the news must have been for her. Finding Christopher meant everything to her, but she didn't want to do so at the expense of another mother. Maureen was relieved that Jose's mother was happy for the Santora's. Jose's mother firmly believes that her son is in heaven and that he is at peace. She wishes the very same for the Santora family.

Hearing about this exchange between these two mothers was breathtaking and inspiring. Many people have written of love, but I believe Saint Paul best described love in his first letter to the Corinthians:

> Love is patient, love is kind. It is not jealous, love is not pompous, it is not inflated, it is not rude, it does not seek its own interests, it is not quick-tempered, it does not brood over injury, it does not rejoice over wrongdoing but rejoices with the truth. It bears all things, believes all things, hopes all things, endures all things. Love never fails.

These two women are perfect examples of Paul's message. Two strangers shared the same tragedy, yet as mothers, they shared another commonality: love for their sons.

We live in a media-driven world, and the media often chooses to operate in a manner than fails to respect the dignity of the public. When the news of the mistaken identity reached the media, the press flocked to the Santora's' home. It cast a dark pall over the Santora's' home. What should have been comforting news was overshadowed by constant unwanted media presence. For two very private people, the intrusion by the press into their personal lives was bizarre. This violation of their privacy became so intrusive that Maureen was forced to disguise herself to avoid being detected when she entered and left her home. No one ever reported about the media behaving as they did with the Santora's.

The memorial Mass that was originally planned for Christopher Santora was changed to a funeral Mass at Saint Rita's, and it was celebrated on the same date and time as the Santora's had planned for the memorial service. It was a very small step for their personal healing journey, but it was a step toward healing. Being able to have Chris back also gave the family an opportunity to have a place to go visit with him.

Over the course of his career, Al has attended far too many line-of-duty funerals for members of the New York City Fire Department. Those funerals were always well attended by members of the department, and there was always large presence from nearby municipalities. Boston, New Haven, and Philadelphia would send representatives to FDNY funerals. When Chris's funeral procession reached Saint Rita's, Al was filled with admiration. There were firefighters from cities all across the country—and Great Britain, Germany, and Ireland. Al Santora always knew that firefighting was a brotherhood, but he didn't realize that it was a global one. He was filled with a sense of immense pride as he looked over all the assembled firefighters. He appreciated that it was their way of sharing their love for Chris with the family.

The weeks and months after Chris's funeral were extremely

difficult for Al and Maureen. It was the beginning of a journey toward healing. That journey was painful and reflective. It caused them to examine themselves and the world around them. Prayer was a critical component for Maureen, and she readily admits that she couldn't have gotten through that period without her religion. In her prayers, Maureen would ask God to empower her with the strength to go on. She acknowledges that, for those who have doubts about their faith, a tragic event can cause them to give up their faith. In her prayers, she prayed for those who had such doubts.

As a teacher, Maureen had a controlling, results-driven personality. Early on her journey, Maureen fell into the trap of setting a timetable for her healing. When that didn't meet her expectations, she began to struggle with it. She would ultimately come to the conclusion that she needed to work on this with someone. Fundamental to her healing was remaining positive and avoiding negative people. The fire department's chief medical officer, Dr. Kerry Kelly, was very helpful and encouraging. Dr. Kelly stressed that she accentuate positive people and places.

Al's faith was also the key factor in his journey toward healing. He credits his religion as a life rope that he was able to anchor himself to during the darkest hours. Al posed a hypothetical question to me, and it was a question that left me unable to respond: "What would an atheist do if he or she was in the same circumstances?" While Chris was missing, people came up to him, offered him comfort, and told him that his family was in their prayers.

As Al reflects back to that time, he is grateful to all those people. He might not have realized it then, but their outpouring of love was a significant gift. He feels that this was the work of the Holy Spirit reaching out to him and his family. Al admits that the random acts of kindness that he and his family experienced were greatly appreciated, and they reminded him that we are never alone. When he speaks of his journey, he admits that it took some time and required him to learn how to cope with the pain. Through a good deal of effort and the passage of time, some of the pain has waned.

Maureen and Al both highlight that Christopher's death was a public death, and as such, it is something that is shared. With any sudden death, particularly with a younger person, there are a number of emotions that come into play for family members. Guilt and assuming undeserved responsibility are common responses that can increase the stress of those who are grieving.

The events of 9/11 took on a special meaning for a nation, and as a nation, we collectively mourn and remember on that date. The Santora's and many other families find themselves being placed under the lens of the media when the anniversary of September 11 comes around. This is not a common occurrence to most people who have lost a loved one. It is unique to the families who perished that day. Finding themselves in the public's eye again adds another layer of stress to the family members.

Sharing is very important to Maureen and Al, and their journey toward healing was similar to everything else in their lives. It was a joint venture. The Santora's were active participants in the FDNY's parents' group. It was a much-needed and much-appreciated program. For the Santora's, having the ability to share their daily experiences and challenges with others who were going through the same struggles proved to be a big help in the healing process. They continue to hold a great deal of admiration for the FDNY counseling unit. They know all the different families that the unit cared for, and they are thankful for the counseling unit's willingness to share information with the families.

The Santora's decided that they could best honor Chris by keeping his memory alive and being of service in his name. They have risen to the challenge and are involved in a full array of projects. Al and Maureen serve as active representatives in the National Fallen Firefighters Association. Whenever they are given an opportunity to address members from that organization, they both highlight the excellent work of the FDNY counseling unit. They encourage other fire departments around the country to use the FDNY as an example of a proactive response to its members and their families.

Al and Maureen have taken on other roles with the National Fallen Firefighters Association. They addressed the families of nineteen firefighters (smokejumpers) from Arizona who were killed in the line of duty. They were given the opportunity to interact with family members, shared their common losses, and offered encouragement and guidance. They both are honored to sit on the FDNY's advisory board for line-of-duty deaths. Through this committee, both Al and Maureen are afforded the venue to share their personal experiences with others who have also suffered similar losses. Through their efforts, they are able to ensure that all the necessary resources are available and in place for the families of future line-of-duty deaths.

The Santora's played an instrumental part in the establishment of the Queens Firefighters Memorial at Saint Michael's Cemetery. They worked with local elected officials and local community groups to see this memorial become a reality. This inspiring memorial acknowledges the sacrifices of the firefighters who worked or lived in Queens and died on that fateful day. It also provides family members and members of the general public a place to quietly reflect upon the sacrifices made on that day.

In 2011, as a way of honoring Christopher's sacrifice, Maureen launched the Honor 9/11 Heroes Memorial Tour. In September, to commemorate the tenth anniversary of 9/11, Maureen conducted a series of speaking engagements, press interviews, and memorial event appearances. The primary goal of the tour was to honor the memory of all September 11 fallen heroes by raising money for the Honor 9/11 Heroes Literacy Drive, which seeks to donate five thousand copies of The Day the Towers Fell and My Son Christopher to NYC elementary schoolchildren.

In September of that year, Maureen and Al received a special honor rarely granted to civilians, and it is something they greatly cherish. That honor was being invited to travel aboard the USS New York on its journey to Manhattan for the tenth anniversary of the 9/11 terrorist attacks.

Thanks to the efforts of Senator Charles E. Schumer, the United States Navy agreed to return the USS New York to her namesake to mark the tenth anniversary of the attacks. "It just didn't make sense for this powerful and awesome demonstration of American strength, born out of the rubble of 9/11, not to be present for the tenth anniversary ceremonies," said Schumer. "Over seven tons of steel from the World Trade Center were used to construct this ship, and its return home makes good on its motto: 'Never forget.'" The Santora's were welcomed aboard the USS New York at her home port in Norfolk, Virginia, on September 5, 2011, and they arrived in Manhattan on September 8.

The New York City Board of Education has also honored the sacrifice of Christopher Santora by naming a public school after him. On September 7, 2002, the Firefighter Christopher A. Santora School PS 222Q in the Jackson Heights neighborhood of Queens opened its doors to its students. Their school motto is "Inspiring greatness—one child at a time." The students need only to look at the name over the school doors for inspiration. One of the yearly events at the school is the 9/11 commemorative walk. On the day of the walk, the students hold an American flag and wear a firefighter's hat and Christopher's T-shirt. It is a solemn day imbued with the spirit of hope, courage, and resiliency—the American way!

As a lifelong educator in the New York City school system, one passion that Maureen holds very dear is literacy. To help foster literacy and promote learning, Al and Maureen have created the Christopher Santora Educational Scholarship Fund. This fund grants $50,000 in scholarships each year to New York City students. The awards are given to elementary school, middle school, and senior high school students. The fund is dedicated to the continuing education of young American students from all walks of life that have something special about them as well. Not all of the scholarship winners are at the top of their classes. The intent of the awards is to represent the broadest spectrum possible. There are only two requirements for scholarship winners. They must be American citizens and must respond with a well-written essay to a question posed about a person or event in American history.

Al and Maureen have traveled many of life's paths together, and this journey was the hardest. They will never be without the pain of the loss of their beloved Christopher, but they know that they will meet him one day—and that eases some of the grief. Christopher Santora was a bright and gifted young man. He had his whole future before him, and that future was as bright as the day he died. However, the memory of Christopher did not die that day. Maureen and Al have worked tirelessly to keep their son's memory alive—and they continue to do so.

6

Firefighter Thomas J. Hetzel FDNY

*Whoever possesses God in their being has Him
in a divine manner, and He shines out to them in
all things; for them all things taste of God and in
all things it is God's image that they see.*
Meister Eckhart

Thomas J. Hetzel was one of four children born to Egon and Barbara Hetzel. The family had established its roots in the neatly manicured community of Garden City South on Long Island. From an early age, it became obvious to his parents that Thomas was infatuated with the fire department. Tom's favorite toy was his collection of fire trucks, and they were never very far from his side. His family members recall how, at age five, Tom decided to paint his bike fire engine red. He was a regular fixture in the neighborhood, racing up and down the sidewalk on that bike whenever he heard the sound of the sirens. Those sirens filled him up with an ardent fervor that would eventually propel him to join the volunteer fire service in his local community. Egon remembers a poster in Tom's room of a fireman carrying a child out of a fire. It was apparent that this was going to be his career path.

Tom attended Saint Thomas the Apostle Grammar School in nearby West Hempstead. After completing his studies at

Saint Thomas, he went on to graduate from Carey High School in Franklin Square. Although he didn't think of himself as a serious student, he instinctively knew he should continue his studies. He went on to further his education by studying liberal arts at Nassau Community College.

Early on, Tom became completely absorbed by sports. It really didn't matter what the game was—he threw himself into every competition with all that he possessed. As he grew, he developed a passion for skiing that would compel him to travel to Colorado every year to enjoy the slopes. His love of skiing would also take him to the Alps where he honed this special talent even more. Thomas also developed a keen interest in the sport of European handball, and he became extremely proficient in it. The game's history can be traced back to his family's homeland of Germany. Tom was so gifted in European handball that he earned a place on two United States Junior Olympic teams.

Egon retired as an operating engineer and was an extremely resourceful and knowledgeable man in building construction. As a young boy, Tom helped him with a number of projects around the house. Egon enjoyed sharing his knowledge of construction and mechanics with his son. Tom was a quick learner and he developed a keen eye for detail. Tom's natural mechanical talents coupled with his attention to detail would cause to him to be accepted into the apprenticeship program in Local 3 of the International Brotherhood of Electrical Workers. He would continue to work as a union electrician until his appointment to the New York City Fire Department.

When Thomas turned eighteen, he joined the Franklin Square Fire Department, and he remained a member for the rest of his life. It was a natural progression for a young man who was consumed by the fire service. Once he had become a member of the volunteer fire service, it became apparent that Tom had discovered his true niche in life. Past and present members of his volunteer firehouses all agree that Tom Hetzel was a very special person who brought a great deal of energy, enthusiasm, and talent to the fire service. Those attributes earned him the respect and admiration of his fellow firefighters. His desire to learn as much as he could about the fire service made him an asset to any fire company. During his tenure with the Franklin Square Fire Department, it became evident that Tom was a natural leader in the fire service. All his peers readily acknowledged his gift. While he was a member of the Franklin Square Fire Department, he reached the conclusion that he wanted to become a member of the New York City Fire Department.

Tom carried that same enthusiasm and passion for everything he ever undertook. If he heard that a friend or a neighbor was painting his or her house, he would predictably be the first one at the house with his own paintbrush. After Tom perished, Barbara and Egon were inundated with people who told them of countless acts of kindness that Tom had rendered for them.

To this day, they remain mesmerized by the sheer number of people's lives that he was able to have a positive influence on. They find it even more remarkable that he was able to reach so many people in such a short lifetime. In a world where many people live self-centered lives, Tom's kind and giving nature was a breath of fresh air.

Not long after he was in the electrician's union, Tom took the firefighter examination with the FDNY. For him, it was not a job offer or a position. Tom viewed it as a calling that presented him the opportunity for a lifetime commitment to helping others. By that time, he had discovered that becoming a member of the New York City Fire Department was what he was truly called to be. He felt that being a part of the FDNY also presented him with the prospect of responding to an assortment of fires and emergencies unlike any other. After successfully passing the written and physical components of the test, Tom was placed on the civil service list for firefighter with the FDNY. Being placed on this list is the first step in a lengthy process prior to being appointed to the department. Tom knew this, and much like every other candidate, he just waited for the call. When he received the call, he was ordered to report to the probationary firefighter school on Randall's Island.

When Tom received his notice of appointment letter, he was thrilled beyond words. He couldn't wait to begin this new journey on his life path. However, not everyone in the Hetzel household was as eager to see Tom join the FDNY. His mother had a great deal of trepidation about seeing her son enter what she felt was a very dangerous profession. Tom reassured her that he would always use caution when he was at work. Eventually, Tom was able to convince his mother that he would be safe in his new career.

After he completed his probationary training, Tom was assigned to Ladder Company 13. Ladder Company 13 is quartered with Engine Company 22 on Eighty-Fifth Street on the Upper East Side of Manhattan. Ladder 13's response area is an extremely unique one. That part of the city is comprised of an assortment of buildings with different forms of construction, and it contains a diverse occupancy too. Ladder 13 is called to respond to high-rise office and apartment buildings, commercial buildings and stores, and tenement buildings in nearby Harlem. It was an ideal environment for a young firefighter to be exposed to, and it offered a distinctive backdrop for a young firefighter to learn about firefighting. Tom was overjoyed about being a member of such an elite company; he eagerly looked forward to each and every tour of duty.

Tom was extremely proud of his German heritage, and he enjoyed listening to German music and attending German festivals. His warm manner and good sense of humor made him quick friends with all the members of Ladder 13. Soon after he was assigned to the company, he developed a passion for cooking, especially in the firehouse, and he became famous for preparing many German dishes for the members of his company.

Just prior to 9/11, Tom received a commendation from the department because of his efforts in helping motorists during a major flood on East River Drive. He had begun to study in preparation for the upcoming lieutenant's examination. Tom relished every moment in the FDNY. He had confidence that it was time to advance in his career.

Not long after he was appointed to Ladder 13, Tom met someone who would change his life forever. He would fall in love with Diana and eventually go on to marry her. They were a perfect couple and shared many interests. After their marriage, they decided to settle down in the town of Elmont on Long Island. Diana shared the same passion for skiing, and they made a yearly ritual of visiting Colorado and hitting the slopes of the Rocky Mountains.

Tom once worked all night to help get the lights back on for a flower shop owner. When the owner asked what he could pay him, Tom said he just wanted roses to take to Diana. Their special union would produce a daughter. Amanda was only two on that tragic September morning. Tom's family members recall how proud he was to be a father and how much of a positive influence Amanda had in his life. They fondly remember him being in a good place and how his life had taken on a new and deeper sense of purpose.

Another characteristic that Tom had been blessed with was his reliability. His word was his bond, and he always followed through on whatever he said he would do. The week before September 11, Tom's family went on a cruise to Russia. Tom and Diana were invited, but they declined so that Tom could continue studying for the lieutenant's promotional examination. Barbara was concerned about leaving a sick relative at home, but Tom promised he would look in on her. When the family returned, Barbara learned that he had checked in on that relative. She also noticed that her car was detailed because Tom said it needed it and that he would do it. Egon had needed to place a shelf up in the house. When he returned, he noticed that his son had already completed the task. Tom's brother had lent him a pair of rollerblades to use prior to the trip. He told Dan that they needed new rollers, and when Dan returned from the cruise, he found the rollerblades hanging in the garage with the new rollers installed on them.

The Christmas before 9/11, Tom had taken Amanda to a photography studio. He had posed for a photograph while wearing his fire bunker clothing and holding his precious Amanda in his arms. This picture mirrored the poster that had hung in his bedroom when he was a child. That Christmas, all of Tom's friends and family received copies of that photo. All his friends and family still cherish it dearly. When Egon looks at that picture of his son, he is elated by it, knowing the wonderful husband and father that his son had become.

On the morning of September 11, 2001, Thomas Hetzel was on duty with Ladder Company 13. Tom's company would respond to the World Trade Center along with Engine Company 22. Ladder Company 13 was assigned to assist in the search and rescue operations in the North Tower. Tragically, Tom and eight other brave firefighters from that firehouse would perish that morning. Tom Hetzel had been with the FDNY for five years, and he left a loving wife and daughter.

Outside that Upper East Side firehouse, there is a memorial with the photos of the nine firefighters who were lost that day. It bears the following inscription: "There was a time when the world asked ordinary men to do extraordinary things: September 11, 2001."

BARBARA AND EGON HETZEL

When each partner loves so completely that he has
forgotten to ask himself whether or not he is loved in
return; when he only knows that he loves and is moving
to its music—then and then only are two people able
to dance perfectly in tune to the same rhythm.
Anne Morrow Lindbergh, Gift from the Sea

Thomas Hetzel grew up on Kilburn Road in Garden City South. As I turned onto that street I noticed another sign on the street post. That sign indicated that the street had been renamed Firefighter Thomas J. Hetzel Road. Egon Hetzel recalls the day his block was dedicated in his son's honor, and he beams with pride. That day, the street was filled with many dignitaries and a host of friends and family. They all gathered to pay their respects to the town's hero firefighter. He adds that the dedication acknowledges Tom's sacrifice on September 11, 2001, and his lifelong dedication to his local community.

On the morning of September 11, 2001, the Hetzel family (except for Tom, Diana, and Amanda) was on the cruise in Europe. Being on a ship that was so far away from home, the news of the events surrounding the World Trade Center was not as detailed as what people in America were experiencing. They received some limited information from the BBC, but it was not anything similar to the type of coverage that the American media was providing. Diana told Barbara and Egon that Tom had responded to the fire and was listed among the unaccounted for. The entire family was overwrought, and given the fact that they were so far from home, they began to feel helpless.

In the days that immediately followed September 11, the restrictions on travel of any kind were unlike any ever seen before. The Hetzel family needed to get home and be with Diana and Amanda. In the hours after 9/11, many people across America witnessed random acts of kindness. There was a genuine concern for people who were affected by this tragedy—and even for those who weren't. The aftermath of 9/11 presented the world with an opportunity to become more contemplative and reflective of what truly mattered to them. Life slowed down, and people stopped to take notice of the things and people around them. The Hetzel family witnessed this phenomenon from thousands of miles away.

When the administrative personnel of the cruise line became aware of the situation that presented itself to the Hetzel's, they took immediate actions to expedite their journey home. All the airline carriers who were involved did all that they could to assist the family in every possible way. Everywhere along their trip home, people extended themselves and offered their sympathies to the Hetzel's. The family still is in awe of the consideration that befell them and remains grateful for all that was done for them. A woman at the airport gave Barbara five hundred dollars and a pair of wooden shoes for Diana and Amanda. Barbara felt that the woman was an angel who was trying to ease her grief.

When the Hetzel's returned home, they couldn't believe the devastation at what had been the World Trade Center. With Diana, they began to hope and pray that a miracle might present itself. Finally, after several weeks of searching, Thomas's remains were recovered amid the twisted steel and crumbled concrete that was once the North Tower of the World Trade Center. He was found beside the other members of his company. On October 9, 2001, a funeral Mass was offered for him on Long Island. Immediately following, Thomas Hetzel was laid to rest. He was buried with full honors by the FDNY, and the amount of people in attendance was massive. The sight of so many people in attendance reinforced for Barbara and Egon the reality of just how many lives their brave young son had affected.

Kilburn Road in Garden City South is no stranger to tragedy. In 1972, a young girl was killed when a car jumped the curb and struck her. That precious little girl was named Christine Hetzel. The loss of Christine shattered the Hetzel family, and they struggled to find answers to their heartbreak. When Christine died, many of the support measures and groups that exist today hadn't been thought of. Much of what we have learned about grief and the grieving process hadn't been developed at the time. She was advised by doctors to "just get on with your life." After a time of long and deep reflection and prayer, Barbara and Egon began to move toward some healing.

Barbara also remembers how great an impact the loss of Christine had on Thomas. The young boy was greatly troubled by this tragedy, and he couldn't make any sense out of it. He missed his sister dearly and wanted to know why that terrible thing happened to her. Thomas's parents knew and felt exactly as he did. They couldn't make any sense out of it either. The doctors would advise the Hetzel's not to put fear into Tom. Tom did have fear, but it was from the reality of that tragic event. For the Hetzel's, it was a double-edged sword of the loss of a child and witnessing the grief it brought to a surviving sibling. They had something to offer Tom and to each other: love. They were blessed to be a strong and loving family who could easily communicate with each other. They admit that it was a long and troubled period, but having the love of each other helped a great deal. Their faith in God would also prove to be a critical component on their journey.

Everyone deals and copes with grief in his or her own way, and no one way is the right or wrong way. Each person must find his or her own way through troubled waters. Men and women cope with stress and tragedies in different ways, and Barbara and Egon are not exceptions to that. The loss of a second child was a devastating blow to Barbara and Egon, and it left them even more shocked and confused. For the Hetzel's, dealing with the loss of their son was an overwhelming tragedy, and it stirred up an array of other emotions. Egon felt more comfortable sharing his feelings with Barbara. Barbara needed to share her feelings and thoughts with Egon and someone else. Their love for each other was manifested in the support and respect that they shared for each other's decision to approach grief in different ways.

Barbara joined the FDNY's parents' group at the Freeport firehouse, and she was a regular attendee of the group's Thursday night meetings. The group was a gift, and she was thankful for the group leaders, Gerry and Trudy. Barbara was impressed with the many commonalities she shared with the other parents. She was impressed with values that all the sons had shared with each other. Although she knew no one in the group, she quickly developed new and deep friendships with the other parents. She is still in contact with many of the parents, and she often sees many of them on a social level. She deeply appreciates that she can call any member of the group when she needs to talk, and she is equally appreciative that she can be of assistance to other members of the group.

At some of the Thursday night meetings, no one spoke. At some, everyone cried. It was always a shared experience for the parents.

Barbara said, "Some nights were bad, some were good, but we were there to help each other." Her faith would be tested again with the loss of Tom, and it would take her longer to accept it on a spiritual and emotional level than it did with Christine. Slowly, she and Egon would move forward, but nothing would ever erase their grief. Egon and Barbara share a reference to a timeline that many of the parents from the group cite. They reference that timeline as either "before 9/11" or "after 9/11." For all the parents, spouses, family members, and friends of those lost at the World Trade Center, the world was turned upside down—and their personal reference point will always be that horrific day.

When Barbara looks at the events of 9/11, she struggles with the issues from an intellectual perspective. Barbara was born in Germany, and as a small child, she witnessed the ravages of war. She saw the concentration camps that were used to eliminate millions of people from throughout Europe. Dictatorship and blind fanaticism led a nation to believe and act in the annihilation of people because of religion or culture. She is troubled by current events in the world, and she is concerned for her children and grandchildren. Barbara continues to be resilient, and she is hopeful that history won't repeat itself. In her prayers, she asks that her children and grandchildren live in a world filled with peace. She believes that "life somehow circles back to the good things." Barbara has been blessed with an abundance of hope, and it shines through her like a beacon.

Barbara and Egon miss Tom dearly. They take comfort in knowing that he was a good son, husband, father, and sibling. They know he was a gifted and caring person who was blessed with the ability to tune into and connect with people. They are very proud that his final act was saving people. Egon told me of an encounter that he experienced with a survivor who was in the towers that morning. The man was in the elevator with Tom when the building's power went out. The elevator came to an abrupt halt, and Tom instinctively reached down to the floor of the unlit elevator car, picked up his tools, and forced the doors open—all in the dark. The car was at a floor landing, and everyone was able to then proceed to a stairwell.

Egon becomes filled with pride when he speaks of his son's bravery. He said it was "typical for Tom to always remain calm and take the appropriate measures to remedy the situation." He added that, even as a very young boy, "Tom would take a methodical approach to almost every undertaking or problem that he would encounter."

Barbara and Egon are deeply saddened that their son's life was taken so soon. They agree that his future would have been filled with many more wonderful accomplishments. The Hetzel's look at Tom as a precious gift, and they are thankful for the little time they were blessed with him. The linchpin in their healing journey was their love of each other and the support and love from their family. Their mutual love of family permeates the room, and it becomes apparent that—as a family—they can overcome any challenge. Barbara relishes the moments when she is able to spend time with her family. She speaks fondly of a lifetime of family meals together and rooms being filled with love and laughter. They have shared this genuine love for almost fifty years, and it is as strong today as it was then.

Tom's daughter, Amanda, was recently presented with an award for her studies in German. The Hetzel's know that Tom would have been so proud to witness the ceremony. Tom's love of his heritage was something that his parents were extremely proud of. To honor that love of his heritage, the Hetzel family has created a scholarship in Tom's name at nearby Hofstra University. The Thomas Hetzel Endowed Memorial Award in German Studies is given to a deserving student studying abroad in Germany through a Hofstra-sponsored program or other accredited American university program.

The Hetzel family has dedicated themselves to preserving the memory of Tom for others to be inspired by. They decided that being proactive and positive would best serve and honor his life. In the years since 9/11, the Hetzel family has made numerous contributions to the New York City Firefighters Burn Center in Tom's memory. They have also created an annual memorial gift to the Fisher House Foundation. Fisher House Foundation is best known for a network of comfort homes where military and veteran families can stay at no cost while a loved one is receiving treatment.

7

Firefighter Christopher Pickford FDNY

*Music is a moral law. It gives soul to the universe,
wings to the mind, flight to the imagination, and
charm and gaiety to life and to everything.*
—Plato

In the early 1970s, Americans began to take a serious look at the world in which they lived, and for many, it wasn't a pleasant sight. Pollution coupled with indifference toward the environment was sadly becoming more and more prevalent in American culture. Literary works such as Rachel Carson's *Silent Spring* would help foster a new sense of awareness. This new cognizance would aid in grassroots movements that eventually propelled people into such actions as instituting the first Earth Day in 1970. Ecology proponents began to galvanize, which led to an assortment of programs designed to educate the public about the consequences that we all would face if we didn't rethink our views on the environment. One of the more successful methods of providing the public with this necessary information concerning our environment was through the use of public service messages on television.

Perhaps the most memorable and ironic of these broadcasts employed a Native American man as its spokesperson. The ironic part is that the man never spoke a single word throughout the advertisement. In the video portion, the man is shown paddling his canoe on a pristine stream along a serene uninhabited area. As he continues along his journey, he makes his way along the waterway to an urban center. When the man paddles through the urban area, it becomes obvious that the background is filled with a host of subliminal messages. The pristine waters are gone. An urban waterway is contaminated with debris and an oil slick. In the background, smokestacks from industrial plants are belching acrid emissions. When the man debarks at the shoreline, the camera reveals that it is covered in litter. The camera focuses on the man's back as he surveys the toxic scenery. As the man turns toward the camera, it zooms in on him crying. This public service message was well ahead of its time, and it became the driving force in public awareness for many environmental issues.

On a bright and sunny spring afternoon in Kew Gardens, Queens, Linda Pickford and her four-year-old son are taking a stroll. Christopher is excited to be outside and is filled with curiosity. Curiosity in four year olds often places them where they shouldn't be, and Christopher is no exception. Christopher stoops down and picks up loose pieces of litter that he has discovered on the sidewalk. Linda tries to discourage him by telling him that he could become sick if he continues. Christopher looks somewhat confused by his mother's cautionary advice; nevertheless, he continues to pick up the litter. When Linda warns him again, Christopher says, "I don't want to make the man cry." That exchange remains a Kodak moment for Linda.

That story serves as a window into the type of man Christopher would become. Chris would develop true respect and love for nature. He also nurtured and perfected a concern for humankind in adulthood. Chris loved to plan and organize trips to upstate New York with his friends. Getting out of the city every now and then seemed to put Chris at peace with himself and his surroundings.

Chris Pickford was blessed with a bevy of friends, and they all grew to rely on his organizational skills. Early on, his friends would come to admire and respect his leadership qualities. Chris was a large man who was six foot four. Although his mere presence might appear to be intimidating to those who didn't know him, to his friends, Chris was an affable and lovable gentle giant. Chris's friends nicknamed him "Super." To his circle of friends, he was the glue that held the group together.

Christopher Pickford entered this world on Father's Day. His father would always say that Chris was the greatest Father's Day gift he had ever gotten. Six years later, the Pickford family would be blessed with another son, David. As the two brothers grew, so did the typical sibling rivalries. Chris was always there for David—no matter what the situation was. Being a caring big brother was a role that Chris enjoyed, and he was extremely comfortable in it.

Before his teenage years, Chris discovered his true love: music. Music was the force that fueled his life. Chris would spend hours practicing and writing music. His music also went to define him. Linda remains amazed at this gift that Chris possessed. He was a talented musician and songwriter. In high school, he formed the band Riboflavin and the Vitamin Ds with his schoolmates. Chris would write the music and the lyrics. Chris would form the group Ten Degree Lean, which was his pride and joy. Sadly, Ten Degree Lean was due to record their first full-length album in October 2001, but the events of September 11 precluded that from happening. Those who were familiar with Chris's music agree that it was filled with contemplative and meaningful thoughts. In high school, the band was often looking for a place to practice and develop new songs. Chris was able get the pastor of his parish to let the group use the church basement for some of the sessions. The pastor was able to get Chris to volunteer at a summer camp for underprivileged children. Linda fondly recalls how big an impression that experience made on Chris.

Chris was intrigued by the theater. The theater had fascinated Chris so much that he decided to enroll in theater classes to learn as much as he could about this exciting medium. Being blessed with musical talents, Chris thrived in his theater classes. He wrote a full-length play that was highly received by his classmates and instructors. Christopher Pickford was gifted and talented in so many ways, and his intelligent demeanor funneled those gifts in many positive directions. He was a young man with a bright future in front of him.

Chris had known since he was a child that he wanted to become a New York City firefighter, but becoming a firefighter is a time-consuming process. Chris had a good deal of patience, and he remained determined to become a firefighter. In the meantime, Chris entered Queensboro Community College and graduated. He began working at the Queens County district attorney's office, but without proper certification, advancements were limited. Determined to advance, Chris enrolled in classes at York College and eventually became a certified paralegal. He remained with the district attorney until his appointment to the FDNY. Although it was difficult to leave his many friends and coworkers at the district attorney's office, Chris was overjoyed to become a member of the New York City Fire Department.

After Chris was appointed to the FDNY, he completed his probationary firefighting training at the fire academy on Randall's Island. He was eventually assigned to Ladder Company 136 in the Elmhurst neighborhood of Queens. After his first year on the job, and in keeping with department policy at that time, he was temporally assigned to Engine Company 201 in Brooklyn. Chris was the happiest he had ever been. He had reached his goal, and he was enjoying every minute of it. His easy manner and sense of humor served him well, and he quickly made friends in his new environment.

Chris's size and strength made most of the more strenuous assignments in firefighting appear routine. His supervisors and peers in the firehouse could readily see that Chris was a gifted firefighter who was driven to be the best that he could be. They realized that Chris was a quick learner and a team player—both necessary attributes for the fire service.

On the morning of September 11, 2001, Christopher Pickford and the members of Engine 201 responded to an alarm for a fire at the World Trade Center. Christopher Pickford would make the supreme sacrifice that morning with 342 other brave firefighters. He was just thirty-two and had been a member of the New York City Fire Department for only eighteen months.

LINDA PICKFORD

Dear Chris on Your Birthday
From Mom

Losing myself in mundane thoughts when I remembered that you were lost and my heart falls because

Tuesday came: I go to the places that you loved and search for your message and the answers why

Tuesday came: The friends and loves while you were here are those we hold so dear, yet they too are lost because

Tuesday came: I know you said it would be okay if you were to go in this very way, but I can't help thinking you were just being my hero, as always, long before.

Linda Pickford
Chris's Thirty-Third Birthday: June 15, 2002

***

It is a bright and cloudless September morning, and Linda Pickford is at work as a paralegal in the Queens County district attorney's office. Linda begins to notice an unusual buzz in the office, and as she looks around, she notices large numbers of her coworkers watching the few television sets in the office. When Linda moves over to see what everyone is glued in on, she sees that the North Tower of the World Trade Center is engulfed in flames. Linda observes that the newscasters' voices are filled with apprehension as they explain to the audience that a commercial airline plane struck the tower.

Linda is overcome with a frightening sensation as she realizes that Chris is on duty. She calls his firehouse and is somewhat relieved when she learns that he is there. That relief is short-lived as Chris tells her that they expect to be called to the fire any minute. Linda kiddingly tells Chris to tell his lieutenant "that his mother won't let him go." Chris reassures her that everything is all right and that he will be perfectly fine, and they say good-bye. That will be the last conversation that Linda will have with Chris. Moments later, Chris Pickford and Brooklyn's Engine Company 201 are racing toward the World Trade Center. For four of the firefighters from Engine 201, it will be their final response.

Later that Tuesday evening, Thomas and Linda Pickford received the tragic news that Christopher had been listed among those unaccounted for. In those initial hours, Linda recalls how Thomas and she were in a complete state of confusion. Nothing in their lifetimes had ever prepared them for such tragic news. They were desperately searching for answers to questions that no one has the answers to. They began to pray for a miracle, some slight ray of hope, or anything to latch onto. They hear that people might have survived by becoming trapped in a void left from a collapsing tower.

Not knowing anything adds to the stressful situation and also it heightens the anxiety. The Pickford's were filled with anguish. Everything in the world is out of their control, and it is not a feeling that they are comfortable with. Much of the first few hours remain a blur for Linda. At the Pickford home, an unending stream of Chris's friends and fellow firefighters offer support. Relatives and neighbors bring food, prayers, and condolences. Linda painfully recalls her inability to make any sense out of it. It all still seems so surreal to her.

Linda is not satisfied to stay at home and wait for news. She is compelled to action, hoping to find some answers. She is determined to visit the site and see the devastation. On Thursday morning, the Pickford's make their way down to the site that once was home to the World Trade Center. They are the first family to do so.

Upon their arrival at the site, Thomas and Linda begin to face the harsh reality that the chances of anyone being alive are microscopic. The grave images that the Pickford's had observed still cause grief for Linda. They return to the site often though; in some strange way, visiting seems to help. It gives them something to do, and it is far better than sitting at home and waiting for the bell to ring. As the days turn into weeks and the weeks turn into months, the stress continues to mount. Hope is fading. While visiting the site, the Pickford's twice witness a recovery of someone in the collapse zone.

Thomas Pickford is heartbroken as he makes arrangements for a memorial service for his firstborn son. Thomas could always call on Chris for anything. He was so proud of the man Chris had become: a kind and caring person who was loved and admired by his friends. Thomas's fondest memory of Chris was the day Chris told him he was his best friend. Those are powerful words for a father to hear from his son. Thomas knows that parents shouldn't be burying their children, and it is a difficult task to perform. Thomas believes that this is the first step in the healing process. Linda remains firm in the belief that Chris will be recovered. On December 8, 2001, the Pickford family holds a memorial service for Chris.

On the evening of December 31, 2001, underneath a steel I-beam below what was once the South Tower of the World Trade Center, firefighters located the remains of Christopher Pickford and his comrades from Engine Company 201. December 31 is a special day in the Pickford home since it is Thomas's birthday. Finding Chris is a cathartic experience for Thomas and Linda. They are both greatly relieved to have their son back. He can finally be laid to rest.

The Pickford's know they are fortunate to have been able to recover Chris. All around them, they witness so many families who will never find their loved ones. Linda is still greatly troubled for those families who lost someone whose remains were never recovered. Her heart pines for those who are forced to suffer through those tragedies. I find it inspiring that a mother who has lost her son in the midst of this horrific event can lovingly embrace the pain that another family is enduring. I know that the world would be a better place if we all felt about each other as Linda does.

In the aftermath of Chris's funeral, Thomas and Linda remain heartbroken. Linda does her best to hide her feelings. She is greatly concerned that her family will worry too much about her, and the last thing Linda wants is pity. Linda is hesitant to join a group such as the counseling services unit, but Thomas insists that they join. Joining groups isn't something that Thomas Pickford would normally do, and taking part in a bereavement group is something that Linda would never have expected from Thomas. She knows exactly the pain and torture that Thomas is suffering since she feels it too, and she is more than willing to make any sacrifice to help ease Thomas's grief.

After a few of these meetings, the Pickford's begin to experience a sense of peacefulness. Much to Linda's surprise, Thomas begins to vocalize his feelings. Linda begins to feel safe and comfortable with the other members of the group. The Pickford's—like all the members of the group—don't know each other. This family group is a critical component for Linda and Thomas's road to healing. Through the group, Linda and Thomas develop lasting and loving relationships with their fellow parents. More than twelve years removed from their first meeting, Linda still maintains relationships with group members. Frequent phone calls and lunch dates with other parents remind Linda that she is not alone on her journey. Linda realizes that no support group or any amount of counseling can erase her grief, but being with others who were enduring the same sorrow provides her with a great deal of comfort.

The family group meetings enable Linda to witness a side of Thomas that she had never really seen before. Thomas was always the shy and reserved type and had a natural tendency to keep his feelings and emotions to himself. The support from the group empowers him to share the sentiments he is experiencing with others in the group.

Linda vividly recalls Thomas's concern for the single parents in the group and their inability to lean on a spouse in those dark hours. The family support group gave Thomas an insider's view into the dynamics of the fire department family. Thomas would quickly grow to love his son's fire department and its family members. When Linda thinks back to her time with the group she recalls the grief, but she remembers many positive moments as well. The group would help Linda remember that she is not alone and that she is greatly loved and needed. Although she lost Thomas three years after Chris, she is blessed to have David and his lovely wife, Rosemarie. That union has produced two grandsons—Christopher and Peter, their eldest son bears his late uncle's name.

Linda's faith was tested. Linda had always thought that by living the right way—going to church, praying, helping the poor, and being nice to everyone—would result in good things. Why did this terrible tragedy fall on her? It was a question that theologians such as Thomas Aquinas would struggle with as well.

Linda would wrestle with her faith for more than a year after Chris's death, searching for a deeper understanding. Linda eventually concluded that, when we are faced with tragedy, our naïve conceptions sometimes come to the forefront. Through prayer and reflection, Linda has experienced a maturing and deepening of her faith. She is extremely grateful for this growth in her faith, and it has become a constant companion for her. She now takes every day as a gift, and she continues to be thankful for her family and friends whose constant support has meant so much to her. Linda's deeper faith has enabled her to change her worldview too. That deeper faith empowers her to remain cognizant and prayerful for all of humanity. Linda remains cautiously mindful of the fact that we live in an ever-threatened world, and that terrorism is a constant threat.

The Pickford family has remained resolute in perpetuating Chris's story and his sacrifice. Linda is actively engaged in raising funds for the Wounded Warrior Project in Chris's name. Her heart is greatly moved by the dedication and sacrifices that these brave men and women have made to our country. Linda is honored and thankful for the opportunity to reach out to our service members. Chris's brother, David, is also a member of the FDNY, although he never thought too much about becoming a firefighter before September 11, 2001. After he witnessed the outpouring of affection for Chris from his fellow firefighters, David knew where he belonged. David was mesmerized by the unity and the esprit de corps that he witnessed among Chris's fire department colleagues.

Chris wasn't the only Pickford who was blessed with a musical gift. David has taken Chris's songs and arranged them on a CD. The CD also includes some selections that David wrote in Chris's memory. David has sold this CD in Chris's honor, and all the proceeds are given to aid children with autism. This CD has provided the Pickford's with a viable means of preserving Chris's music forever.

Chris Pickford has passed, but his music remains as loud today as it did before September 11. His warmth and kindness live on in the friends he made and the lives he touched in his short life. He will always remain in Linda's life and her heart.

8

Firefighter George Cain FDNY

Now he walks in quiet solitude,
The forests and the streams, seeking
grace in every step he takes,
His sight has turned inside,
Himself to try and understand,
The serenity of a clear blue mountain lake,
The Colorado Rocky Mountain high,
I've seen it rainin' fire in the sky.

George Cain was born in Rockaway Beach, New York, on the May 13, 1966, and he was raised in the Long Island community of Massapequa. As he grew, he would come to be affectionately called Georgie by family and close friends. George was the third child in the Cain family, joining his sister Nancy and brother Dan. Two years later, Erin would be welcomed into the family. At Massapequa High School, George skated for the ice hockey team and played soccer.

As a young boy, George began to exhibit signs of an independent and adventurous personality. Those traits led him to develop an intimate appreciation for nature and the environment. While he was in high school, he learned to ski and immediately fell in love with it. Skiing soon became a passion that consumed him, and it was something he continued to enjoy into adulthood. After he graduated from high school, George began working as a carpenter. He worked tirelessly to hone his carpentry skills and eventually became a skilled craftsman. This evolutionary process enabled him to grasp a deep understanding and appreciation for the other skilled trades in the construction business.

George's innate sense of adventure coupled with his love of skiing would bring him to relocate to Telluride, Colorado. In Colorado, he was at peace with nature and the beauty that the Rocky Mountains offered. It also afforded him instant access to some of the best skiing in the world. As George matured, so did his appreciation for nature and the outdoors. The Rocky Mountains provided a panoramic overview unlike anything he had witnessed before. Prior to leaving New York, George had taken the test to become a New York City firefighter. Becoming a member of FDNY was something that George had always wanted to accomplish. He had realized that it would take some time for a list of candidates to be promulgated—and even more time before any hiring would begin. In the meantime, he was thrilled to have the chance to work and play in such a beautiful part of America.

George earned a good living in Colorado as a carpenter for a construction firm that specialized in building log cabin homes. He worked hard during the warmer months, but once the snow began to fall, he was off to the ski trails. Colorado also provided George with the milieu to satisfy some of his other daredevil impulses. George experienced the thrill of bungee jumping, skydiving, and heli-skiing.

In April 1994, George Cain was appointed to the New York City Fire Department, and he was assigned to Ladder Company 7. Ladder 7 is located in the Kips Bay neighborhood of Manhattan on East Twenty-Ninth Street. George immediately enjoyed being a firefighter and being a member of a team. His knowledge of building construction enabled him to quickly grasp many of the inherent dangers that firefighters face on a daily basis.

George was driven to become the best firefighter that he could be, and his passion toward this goal resulted in him winning the respect and admiration of his fellow firefighters and officers. Through his dedication and work ethic, George quickly became a skilled and knowledgeable firefighter. His sense of humor and love of practical jokes made him an integral member of Ladder 7. George was also very friendly with many of the residents in the community surrounding the firehouse.

George enjoyed camping, and he always had a tent in his truck. George was an avid hiker, and he often took to the trails on his bike. He developed an appreciation for music and was constantly adding to his impressive CD collection. George and his friends were big concertgoers, and George was particular admirer of Jerry Garcia. After he joined the fire department, he took up golf, and much like everything else he did, he embraced it filled with passion. That same passion would propel George to run in the New York City Marathon. George was always attentive to keeping himself in the best physical condition, and he knew it was essential that a firefighter maintain top-notch physical condition at all times. Finishing the New York Marathon with a better than respectable time stands as a testament to just how attentive he was to his conditioning.

George Cain was a confirmed bachelor; marriage and children weren't in his immediate future. He was comfortable with his laid-back lifestyle, and he relished the fact that he could take off on his own or with friends at a moment's notice. The flexible work schedule at the firehouse afforded him all the time off that he needed to be the free spirit that he was. When the situation presented itself, he would go skiing, camping, golfing, or hiking without so much as a second thought. He knew that having a wife and children would no longer afford him the time to enjoy his pastimes. He remained steadfast in his decision to continue to live his life as a single man—at least for the immediate future. In fact, his nickname at the firehouse was "Dude." All the married firefighters at the firehouse were a tad envious of all the personal freedom that he enjoyed. George was blessed with a great sense of humor and was famous in the firehouse for his practical jokes. Humor and ribbing are common in firehouse culture; one must be able to take it as well as give it. George was well versed in both perspectives of this cultural behavior.

George was blessed to have had a very special relationship with his mother. One only needs a few minutes in conversation with Rosemary to grasp the depth of their relationship. Because of the closeness of their birthdays, the Cain family would celebrate George and Rosemary's birthday together. Rosemary and George had even once shared a road trip from Colorado to California. The fond memories of that shared adventure still resonate with Rosemary. She enjoyed George's companionship and humor, and she was able to take deep personal pride in admiring the young man who her son matured into.

Family was always a paramount concern with George. He made it a point to attend every family event. He enjoyed the love and comfort of his family. George basked in the opportunity to spend time with his niece, Meaghan, and nephews, Chris and Conor. He welcomed the time they spent together; he enjoyed being able to teach them how to ski, and he shared his love of camping with them. George embraced his role as Conor's godfather and uncle with the same enthusiasm that he embraced his life. He gave his niece and nephews his time and his love—gifts that they continue to cherish in their memories of him. Whether it was on the ski slopes or playing a simple game with them at a family barbeque, they knew they were special when their Uncle Georgie was around.

Rosemary Cain is blessed to have many family mementos. One of those mementos is a vast collection of photographs of her children and grandchildren. Many of these pictures chronicle George at different events and stages of his life, and in all the photos, he has a discernible grin that gives the viewer a clearer insight into the persona of George Cain. There is a grin of achievement and personal satisfaction as he crossed the finish line at the New York City Marathon. A picture of him in Colorado with a broad smile tells one of the serenity and peacefulness he discovered while he stands with the Rocky Mountains behind him. George's love of family is best manifested by his grin, which is filled with love and intimacy as he poses with his mother and siblings. His love of family permeates the family portraits. Perhaps the most telling of all George's grins is shared in the photographs of him with his niece and nephews. Those photos portray George with an aura around him, showing him experiencing great tranquility and loving every precious moment he was able to spend with the younger members of the Cain family.

On the evening of September 10, 2001, George was on duty with Ladder 7 and was scheduled to be relieved at nine o'clock the following morning. That evening, George's sister happened to be in Manhattan on business and stopped by the firehouse to visit her brother. While Erin was visiting, George invited Erin to stay and have supper with him and the firefighters who were working that night. After dinner, George and Erin spent some time catching up on all the current events in their lives. Erin left the firehouse late that evening, happy that she was able to spend some time with her big brother. Sadly, that would be the last time anyone from the Cain family would see their beloved George.

On the morning of September 11, 2001, Ladder 7 was returning to the firehouse after an alarm when they learned via the department radio that a plane had struck the North Tower of the World Trade Center. Upon hearing the information, the fire department dispatchers immediately began to muster a massive response of fire department units to the scene. Ladder Company 7 was among one of the first units assigned to respond. The FDNY would initially send more than two hundred units to combat this fire and coordinate in the rescue of tens of thousands of endangered civilians. The operation would become the largest emergency response ever undertaken, and it remained a continuous operation until May 2002.

Official fire reports indicate that Ladder Company 7 was last seen aiding in the evacuation of the Marriott Hotel. The Marriott World Trade Center was a twenty-two-story steel-framed hotel building with 825 rooms. The hotel was connected to the North and South Towers, and many people went through the hotel to get to the Twin Towers. Given the time of day when the attacks took place, it was a logical presumption to believe that the hotel was heavily occupied with both hotel staff and guests. In fact, the Marriott Hotel had more than a thousand guests registered that morning, and a business convention was planned for later that day.

The FDNY's chief officers in command who were present on the scene quickly realized the imminent danger that was threatening the guests and staff in the Marriott, and they immediately took steps to evacuate everyone. The chief officers were faced with a fire condition and a rescue operation unlike any other in the history of humankind. Fortunately, the chiefs on the scene used a proactive approach to initiating an immediate evacuation of the guests and hotel staff. This proved to be a significant tactic. Their tactics coupled with the bravery and professionalism of Ladder 7 and all the other units that operated in the Marriott Hotel that morning ultimately saved hundreds and hundreds of innocent lives.

While the massive evacuation of the Marriott was ongoing, the South Tower of the World Trade Center collapsed onto the hotel. The ensuing results of this collapse would account for the loss of dozens of civilians and dozens of firefighters who were in the process of evacuating the hotel. Tragically, Firefighter George Cain and all five of his comrades from Ladder 7 eventually made the supreme sacrifice in the hotel. George Cain was thirty-five years old and had been a member of the New York City Fire Department for seven years.

ROSEMARY CAIN

*We are all molded and remolded by those who have loved
us, and though that love may pass we remain, nonetheless
their work. No love, no friendship can ever cross the path
of our destiny without leaving some mark upon it forever.*
—Francois Mauriac

Upon hearing the news that her beloved George was on the
FDNY's list of unaccounted for, Rosemary Cain's heart shattered.
That sad news rendered her inconsolable; nothing in her life had
ever compared with this loss. There was a very special chemistry that existed between her and George, and that chemistry
manifested itself as mother and son and as intimate friends.
Rosemary was well aware of the many inherent dangers that
firefighters face, but like so many others with sons or daughters
or husbands or wives in the fire service, it was something she
didn't dwell on. It is a reality that all are cognizant of, yet it is a
subject that is never open for discussion.

Rosemary initially found herself engaged in deep prayer,
asking and hoping that George would be found. She prayed for a
miracle. Perhaps he was safe in some void underneath the massive tons of twisted steel and crushed concrete. Her first impres-
sions were to wonder if he was cold, hungry, or thirsty. As days
turned into weeks, she disappointedly accepted the reality that
he was not going to found alive. As she struggled with her grief,
Rosemary joined many other parents in the FDNY's counseling
services parent's group. This group would meet every Thursday
evening at the Freeport firehouse on Long Island. Rosemary
found the group to be a critical tool in her healing process. She
echoes the same accolades that all the other parents attribute
to the group, and she remains grateful to the fire department for
responding to their needs.

The world would stop on Thursdays for Rosemary Cain.

Thursday gave her a time and place where she could withdraw from all the stress that was surrounding her. She readily acknowledges how instrumental the group was to her and to all the other parents. For Rosemary, having the opportunity to be among other parents who were experiencing the same grief as she was put her at ease. Sometimes when the group met, no one spoke. They just cried and held each other. Sharing deep feelings with her fellow parents was extremely cathartic for her.

Officially the group has been disbanded, but the members will always be forever united. Many of these parents still remain in close contact with each other, and they have developed close friendships. Rosemary has remained active with many of the parents, and she has both offered and received support and comfort from her fellow parents.

On November 9, 2001, Rosemary had a memorial service for George at Saint William the Abbott Roman Catholic Church. A contributing factor in her decision to proceed with a memorial service for George was her grandchildren. George had truly loved his niece and nephews, and each of them loved their Uncle Georgie. A memorial service might alleviate much of the stress that the youngsters were experiencing.

The memorial did leave an impression on them. Conor would write a book about his uncle. My American Hero features illustrations that he and Meaghan created. Within that text, the children share their intimate relationship with Uncle Georgie and how the tragic events of 9/11 resonated with them.

Through her special relationship with George, Rosemary knew exactly how he felt about life. She instinctively knew that he would never want anyone to feel sorry for him or her. Rosemary Cain is an independent woman of great passion who is not afraid to voice her opinion. She is also a woman who is not afraid to back up those opinions with action either. She realized that she had to do something positive in the aftermath of the terror attacks on 9/11. Rosemary Cain became a volunteer with the Salvation Army and volunteered her services at their tent on Murray Street, adjacent to the World Trade Center. The tent offered coffee and other beverages and food to the countless streams of first responders and construction workers who toiled in the recovery efforts at the site. The tent also provided shelter from the elements and gave refuge for the workers so that they could get some needed rest.

In reflecting upon her service with the Salvation Army Rosemary says, "The entire experience was therapeutic, and it gave me a purpose." Rosemary was also propelled by a strong desire to witness the tragedy for herself. She vividly recalls the passion that she witnessed in the workers she encountered. She readily embraced her role at the site, becoming accustomed to that strange environment. She knew when it was a good day or a bad day. A good day was when someone was recovered, and a bad day was when no one was recovered. The culture that evolved during the recovery stage of the operation was unique in many ways. It would become a culture that a person had to experience to appreciate or understand. One aspect that developed out of that culture was that body language and facial expressions implied much more that spoken words. People didn't talk that much. A somber and solemn pall echoed throughout the site. All the workers on the site respected where they were, and they all felt that it was sacred ground.

Rosemary and her daughters, Nancy and Erin, visited the site often. Many times, they were escorted there by a liaison from George's firehouse. Every visit was a painful journey, and every time they stood on the site, they would say a fervent prayer for the recovery of their precious George. Rosemary wanted to do more and felt she could join the many volunteers from the Salvation Army. These wonderful people—many were local residents who had witnessed the attacks—felt the need to serve the many responders and workers who were on the site twenty-four hours a day, seven days a week. The tent was set up with every kind of necessity and facility possible. The tent was staffed by three separate shifts of volunteers who would see to it that whatever might be needed by the workers at the site was available to them at any time. Rosemary's first official day of volunteering was December 31, 2001.

She felt it was important for her to spend New Year's Eve down there with her son. While she was driving down to the site that afternoon for her three to eleven shift, she felt so strongly that it was the day that George would be recovered. Shortly after she arrived at the site, she met with a lieutenant from Engine 16, which was quartered with George's company (Ladder 7). Immediately upon meeting him, she said, "You found George, didn't you?" Because of the strong need for certainty, the FDNY would not confirm her feelings until the next day.

On New Year's Day, the captain of Ladder Company 7 visited Rosemary. He confirmed that George had been recovered the day prior, shortly before Rosemary arrived at the site. The news brought tremendous relief to all of George's family. They could bring him home and lay him to rest. While it was a day of celebrating for so many, for George's family, the beginning of a new year would never be the same. A new journey began for all who loved him, and they were learning to live without their beloved George.

Rosemary was on hand when the last beam was taken down from the World Trade Center. It was a memorable moment for her, and she is grateful that the media wasn't present to intrude upon the dignity associated with the significance of the event. She knows that the media is both a powerful and useful organization, but she feels that sometimes they overstep their boundaries. When the last beam was loaded onto a flatbed truck, the United States Navy participated in an honor guard as it passed. It happened to be fleet week in New York City, and the Navy was more than willing to participate in the event. Seeing all those sailors in dress whites filled Rosemary's heart with pride.

Rosemary is grateful that her George has been found and could finally be laid to rest. The details of George's recovery were in the next day's newspapers, but George's remains were taken to Virginia for DNA forensic identification. The procedure had been implemented to ensure beyond any doubt the correct identity of the person. Because of this procedure, the Cain family couldn't have a funeral Mass for George until March 9, 2002.

Although she was grateful that George had been recovered, Rosemary faced another layer of stress. After people read about George's recovery, they begin to ask where and when his funeral was taking place. Rosemary didn't want to have to continuously explain the reason for the delay to strangers and coworkers. The news of George's recovery was raw, and as an offshoot of the delay, some serious wounds were reopened.

George was officially identified, and the Cain family had a funeral Mass at Saint William the Abbott—the same church were his memorial Mass was held. The service was jointly conducted with the FDNY and was attended by family, friends, and members of the department. Rosemary is eternally grateful that her beloved George was recovered, her heart aches for those families who never experienced a recovery. She visits him regularly at nearby Saint Charles Cemetery, and never a day passes that she doesn't have a thought of George.

For Rosemary Cain, 9/11 is the one defining day in her life. She now perceives her life in two parts: pre-9/11 and post-9/11. Time has eased some pain, but there are wounds that will never heal for her. She acknowledges that she could have easily fallen into depression, but she quickly realizes what George would have said if she had allowed that to happen to her. Rosemary believes that she is obliged to do the very best she can at everything she does. Rosemary embraces the following philosophy on life: "Our gift to our sons is to live our lives for our sons as it is a gift from God, and we are grateful for it."

Rosemary has struggled with George's death, and she

continues to experience the grief of his loss. On an intellectual level, she believes that a normal death is compartmentalized process that moves in a few days and allows healing to begin. A 9/11 death didn't offer the same process. Some bodies were never recovered, and others had both memorials and funerals. Not knowing if their loved ones would be found was a heartbreaking progression that worsened each day. She knows that it is an individual's choice to decide how a person deals with such a loss. She recognizes that there is no right or wrong solution to this complex issue. Having George's name released to the media on New Year's Day and not having his remains available for a proper burial until March placed her under another emotional strain. Rosemary's culture and faith dictates that we bury the dead. Not having an active voice in the DNA process added to that emotional strain. Rosemary and all the parents in the parents' group acknowledge that this tragedy has placed them all under untold layers of stress, and that stress was something that they weren't prepared for.

Holidays and birthdays are particularly stressful for Rosemary—along with every anniversary of September 11. Watching other tragic events occurring around the world evoke feelings of that terrible September day. The media intruded at their loved one's memorials and funerals, and each September 11 creates a sense of unease and a new layer of stress for her and all the parents. George's death—and all those who perished on 9/11—automatically became public. This perspective placed the families under a huge microscope of public examination at what should have been a very private time for them. This scrutiny continues to occur on every anniversary of the attacks on the World Trade Center. Through her time with the parents' group, Rosemary has become empowered with the ability to recognize many of these triggers that set off those stressors. Rosemary realizes that nothing can totally prevent those triggers from occurring, but through the group, she and the other parents are better equipped to handle them.

Soon after the recovery operations concluded, the area that was once the World Trade Center became flooded with onlookers and gawkers. This type of insensitive inquiry troubled many of the families of those who perished. They banded together to do something positive to address the issue. Many family members have acted as docents, sharing the history of the buildings and businesses that were destroyed that day. They also share their loved ones' life stories with the hundreds of thousands of visitors to the site. Their goal is to offer accurate information in a dignified manner that educates all the guests who come to visit.

Rosemary Cain was among the first family members to respond to this pressing need, and she continues to participate as a docent to this day—although not as often as she did in the past. She is happy to have the opportunity to pass on her elaborate knowledge of the tragic events of 9/11 with the guests. She takes great pride in sharing George's story with them too. She also ensures that visitors leave the site with a memorial card with George's photo.

Rosemary is proud of the time she has spent as a docent; she is able to thank the visitors and tell them that their visits are greatly appreciated. A few weeks before Christmas, Rosemary Cain and the other families and volunteers erect and decorate a Christmas tree at Engine 10 and Ladder 10, which is across the street from the old World Trade Center. She hopes to continue this tradition, but she also realizes that she will deeply regret the day that she can no longer erect the tree. Rosemary always volunteers to direct a tour on New Year's Day. Being at the site on the anniversary of the day that George was recovered brings a sense of deep connection with him.

Rosemary Cain is an advocate for the issue of proper burial and for the construction of a fitting above-ground memorial that provides honor and respect. This is an issue that is extremely sensitive to her, and she remains vocal about it. Her goal is to be included in the dialogue and have her voice and all the voices of those who lost loved ones heard. Rosemary believes that the bureaucratic administration of the National 9/11 Museum is insensitive to many of the feelings of the families. She has sought relief from elected public officials in New York City only to be rebuffed by them. Her requests to the hierarchy in the religious congregations in and around the city to intercede on their behalf have only resulted in those officials taking a hands-off approach, preferring to let elected officials resolve the issue.

Rosemary refuses to let her voice and the voices of the other families go unanswered, and she maintains a positive outlook to resolve the issue. Though she is disappointed with some government leaders, she remains as truly loyal and as proud an American as she was prior to 9/11. Her heart is overflowing with pride as she speaks about her grandson, Chris. Chris has completed his second tour of duty in Afghanistan with the United States Army's Tenth Mountain Division. Her disappointment with religious leaders was never over any theological or doctrinal issue. It grew out of the lack of support for a public matter. She believes that religious leaders must speak out on critical issues that face members of their flocks. Rosemary's faith in God is as strong today as it has ever been.

Rosemary and many others with similar views believe that their rights have been usurped by the city of New York. As time passes, they fear that people will grow indifferent and develop a cavalier insight into how this historic site should be cared for. They are not intended to force their opinions or viewpoints on anyone. What is crucial to the families concerned with proper burials is that they want their voices to be heard and acknowledged. They ask that people don't become critical of them if they aren't in their situation. They feel that if everyone reflected on this issue from the same vantage point as the families, there would be a groundswell of support.

George Cain was tragically taken from his family and friends far too early in his life. Fortunately, through the efforts of

Rosemary, her children and grandchildren, and George's friends, he will never be forgotten. The street that he grew up on has been renamed after him to honor his sacrifice. A hiking trail in upstate New York where George loved to hike has been dedicated in his name. A section of his niece and nephews' school library now bears his name with great pride. George's brother, Danny, and his sisters, Nancy and Erin, helped Rosemary organize and run an annual golf outing to honor George's memory. The Cain family ran the outing for ten years after 9/11, and it was well attended and very successful. All the proceeds were donated to High Hopes Therapeutic Riding Academy in Connecticut in George's name. The mission of High Hopes is to improve the lives of people with cognitive, physical, and emotional disabilities through the benefits of therapeutic horseback riding and other equine-assisted activities while serving the therapeutic riding profession through training and education.

Rosemary Cain always carries a prayer card in her purse. On the front of the card is a picture of the late FDNY's Chaplain Mychal Judge OFM. The picture shows Mychal standing along the shoreline and intently looking out to the ocean. Father Mychal was one of the 343 members of the FDNY who made the supreme sacrifice on that September morning. On the back of the card is Mychal's prayer: "Lord, take me where you want me to go, let me meet who you want me to meet, tell me what you want me to say, and keep me out of your way."

Rosemary receives a good deal of comfort when she looks at the card and says Mychal's prayer. His words remind her that we are all in God's hands. The picture of Mychal at the shore is especially meaningful for Rosemary since it brings to mind her childhood in Rockaway Beach, New York. The ocean always fills Rosemary with peaceful thoughts and an inner sense of tranquility. May the Lord continue to guide and hold Rosemary—and may her journey be filled with oceans and oceans.

9

Firefighter Michael Kiefer FDNY

If there is one thing I know for sure in life, it's that God blessed me with the two best parents in the universe! Thanks for raising me with morals and religious values. I love you both.
—Michael Kiefer, Christmas 1996

Most young boys in America dream of becoming many different things while they are growing up. Firefighters, police officers, railroad engineers, or star baseball players are some of the more popular careers that youngsters are fascinated with. As the years pass by, the realities of life begin to settle into our lives. Those realities preclude most of us from ever achieving those goals, and they remain distant memories of youth.

There are very few of us who ever experience the opportunity to fulfill those boyhood aspirations. Michael Vernon Kiefer was one of the few who would become what he had always dreamed about: becoming a New York City Firefighter. Michael came into the world on December 5, 1975. His parents, Pat and Bud Kiefer, were overjoyed. Shortly thereafter, Pat and Bud were equally elated with the birth of his two sisters, Lauren and Kerri.

When Mike was a toddler, Bud recalls taking him to the park and to the firehouse in Franklin Square. Once he entered the firehouse, Mike was immediately mesmerized by the big, shiny, red trucks, and it was not a passing fancy. When Mike was three years old, he announced to his family that he was going to become a firefighter. On the surface, that statement might have sounded similar to a young boy's fantasy. However, for Mike, it was his first step in attaining his lifelong ambition.

Mike developed into an average student who enjoyed playing Little League and soccer. In high school, he joined the swim team. Mike remained passionate about his desire to become a firefighter. He attended Saint Mary's High School in Manhasset, and his yearbook bears this quote: "I want to fulfill my calling and give the best in me." Mike Kiefer was blessed with a deep faith, and Saint Mary's would play a critical role in nurturing Mike's faith formation. Even as a young altar server, Mike's unshakeable faith impressed his parish's pastor. When he tried to recruit him to consider the priesthood, Mike said, "Father, you save the souls—and I'll save the bodies."

As a youngster, Mike began to immerse himself in his pursuit of becoming a New York City firefighter. By the time he was seventeen, he had risen to the rank of captain in the Malverne Junior Fire Department on Long Island. Prior to joining Malverne, he had served with the junior fire department in Franklin Square. Although he wasn't old enough for a drivers' license, Mike would respond to alarms on his bicycle. That was his primary means of transportation. Mike remained in constant contact with the fire department via a radio scanner that kept him abreast of all fire responses in the area. Sometimes, without his parents' knowledge or permission, the calls would take him away from Franklin Square and into areas where he needed a police escort to safely guide him home.

The workload in the Malverne FD didn't present enough opportunities for Mike to satisfy his quest to learn as much about firefighting as he desired. That desire would take him to the Freeport FD and eventually to the Hempstead FD. From his experiences in each of these departments, Mike was able to broaden his knowledge of firefighting and hone the physical and mental skills that are required of firefighters.

Mike's time with the volunteer fire departments helped to broaden his circle of friends. His zeal and enthusiasm made him a desirable asset for any fire company. Throughout his tenure in the volunteer fire service, Mike had numerous opportunities to meet with many members of the FDNY. These were the firefighters who Mike would come to admire and seek out for guidance and direction concerning firefighting. Over the course of a relatively short span of time, Mike would grow many friendships with the members of the FDNY. Through those friendships, he was afforded a panoramic insight into the day-to-day operations of the FDNY. He was friends with the FDNY's chief of department, a former firefighters' union president, the captain of an elite FDNY rescue company, and dozens of other firefighters who worked in various companies throughout the city. The natural approachability in his manner and his ever-present smile made everyone he encountered instant friends.

Mike's faith would continue to grow during that period of his life. He was an active member of his local parish: Saint Catherine of Sienna Roman Catholic Church in Franklin Square. It was the same parish where he had served as an altar server in grammar school. Much like his approach to firefighting, Mike immersed himself in his spiritual life; his personal faith remained a vital part of his life. Besides being a weekly attendee at the liturgy, Mike participated in the celebration of the liturgy. Mike was an extraordinary minister, helping with the distribution of the Sacred Eucharist during Mass. When the need presented itself, he would assist with the greeting and ushering duties in the parish. His fellow parishioners admired him and thought of him as a kind and considerate young man who would always be there to help someone in need.

Mike's swimming abilities enabled him to obtain employment at the town's pool as a lifeguard, and later, he was as a lifeguard for the city of Long Beach. He would often confide in his dad that being a lifeguard at the beach was the second-best job in the world. While working as a lifeguard, he enrolled in classes that would enable him to become a state-certified EMT. Once he became certified, Mike was hired by the FDNY as an EMT. Once he was a certified EMT with the FDNY, Mike was automatically eligible to take the promotion test to become a New York City firefighter. All the pieces of his plan were beginning to fall into place. Mike took the promotion test and received a perfect score on both the written and physical parts. All he had to do was bide his time; to anyone familiar with the civil service system, that wait can be tedious.

Working as an EMT had given Mike his entry into the fire department, yet his goal was still to become a firefighter; all that was left for him now, was to wait for the call. His EMT experience had given him a great deal of exposure to the many medical responses that the FDNY is called for on a daily basis. He experienced a great deal of personal satisfaction in knowing that he was helping those who were in need. It afforded him an opportunity to work in some of the poorer sections of the city, exposing him to a side of the world that he hadn't seen before. If Mike was working on a Sunday, he would park the ambulance outside the nearest church and slip inside for Mass while his partner monitored the radio for calls. His faith remained a fundamental component of his personality, and it helped define him. Mike's religious education in a post-Vatican II world helped enlighten him into the active role that the faithful must play in the liturgy, and it was a role that he embraced.

Mike believed that, as a firefighter, it was necessary to remain physically fit. He embraced his personal conditioning in the same way he embraced everything: passionately. He wanted to be in the best possible shape when he was called to the department. When time permitted between EMS calls, Mike could be found doing push-ups alongside the department ambulance.

Every day when he wasn't working, Mike could be found swimming, running, or bicycling for several hours a day. If there was a 5K or ten-mile race, particularly one sponsored by the fire department, Mike Kiefer would be the first in line to enter. He dutifully maintained a personal training regimen was extremely strenuous. Mike always remained focused on his goal; there was no room for deviation when it came to his conditioning program.

The result of this strict regimen was that Mike had transformed himself into a top-flight triathlete. His approach to his training schedule was similar to that of a professional athlete, and he was always pushing himself to higher levels of physical achievement. His friends would come to admire his achievements, and in return, Mike would offer encouragement to them. Many of his friends were also preparing for the fire department examination, and Mike served as a model for their preparation. Mike wanted the very best for his friends who were also seeking to get "on the job." When he entered the fire department, he was determined to possess all the physical attributes that the job required. From the first day he announced his intentions to join the department; his focus remained on becoming the very best firefighter humanly possible. His experiences in the volunteer fire departments had taught him that firefighting is an extremely physically demanding job, and he was determined to remain physically up to the task.

Pat and Bud Kiefer agree that Mike never presented any discipline issues. Mike was so determined to join the department that he would never act out for the fear that something might jeopardize his chances of being appointed. From an early age, Mike was driven and concerned about his career decision. When he was about ten years old, he had to undergo an emergency appendectomy. His parents recall how nervous and upset Mike was before the operation. He was deeply concerned that the operation might have a negative effect on his chances of becoming a member of the fire department. As an older brother, Mike was always protective of his sisters, cautioning them about the pitfalls that teens face. Lauren and Kerri recall how Mike was always there for them whenever they needed him.

When Mike was called for the fire department, his heart was filled with so much joy that it felt like it was about to burst. Although he possessed a good working knowledge about fire-fighting, Mike kept that to himself. He wanted to learn every-thing and experience everything for himself and not draw any attention to himself in the process. During his tenure in the FDNY probationary firefighter school, Mike was able to develop strong relationships with his classmates. A fundamental aspect of firefighting is teamwork, and the probationary firefighter school stresses the importance of that aspect. Mike's gung-ho attitude and friendly manner made adapting to being a team player easy.

One of the best moments every probationary firefighter ex-periences is without a doubt graduation day, and Mike was no exception to that rule. It is a day filled with personal satisfaction and a time of celebration with friends and family. The Kiefer family was overjoyed to witness Mike as he completed his ar-duous training. He was about to begin his lifelong dream job. At the ceremony, the probationary firefighters were given their permanent assignments at firehouses scattered throughout the city. Mike Kiefer would be assigned to Ladder Company 132 in the Prospect Heights section of Brooklyn. Ladder Company 132 was an extremely active fire company with an excellent reputa-tion; they proudly carried the logo "In the Eye of the Storm." Mike immediately knew that he was very fortunate to have been as-signed to such a prestigious unit, and he was enthusiastic about beginning his firefighting career with Ladder 132.

After he arrived at Ladder 132, Mike settled in to his role as "the Proby." As a Proby, one is expected to be quiet, always keep busy, and never question the status quo. Mike knew this before-hand from his volunteer service and responded in an appropriate manner. His enthusiasm, work ethic, and desire to learn as much as he could did not go unnoticed. His fellow firefighters and officers at Ladder 132 said, "Kiefer is a keeper." Mike Kiefer had made it—just as he predicted to his family twenty-two years earlier. His entire life was in front of him, and he was ecstatic.

On the fateful morning of September 11, 2001, Mike Kiefer was on duty with Brooklyn's Ladder Company 132. Minutes after the first plane struck the North Tower of the World Trade Center, Ladder 132 was assigned to respond to the fire. Six brave firefighters hopped aboard their company apparatus and responded to the site. None of the six would be seen again. Mike Kiefer was just twenty-five years old, and he had been out of the fire academy a mere nine months.

PAT AND BUD KIEFER

Taking a child he placed it in their midst, and putting his arms around it he said to them, "Whoever receives one child such as this in my name, receives me; and whoever receives me, receives not me but the One who sent me."
—Mark 9:37

When Pat and Bud Kiefer received the news that their Mike was listed among the "unaccounted for" by the FDNY they were distraught. They both recall being in a state of total shock, and they remember in the days that followed 9/11 all seemed to have taken on an eerie sense of surrealism. Their lives together had never prepared them for such a horrific event; neither had ever experienced such grief before. Together they had weathered many of the challenges that life presents to all of us, but this was a challenge that they both intrinsically knew would require some assistance. That knowledge would bring them to FDNY's Parents Group, which was a vital component in their personal journeys. Through the efforts of the group the Kiefer's were able to share their grief with others who were suffering the loss; these meetings helped to ease some of their pain.

Bud Kiefer and his son Mike both shared a very special relationship. Not only was he his oldest child and son, but Bud and Mike would grow to become best friends as well. Throughout his life Bud was always there for Mike and Mike was always there for him. One needs to only look into his eyes to appreciate the pain that the loss of a son and a best friend feels like. Although more than a dozen years have passed his heart remains greatly troubled. Sharing his personal grief with the other parents in the FDNY support group and with the group's counselors was very helpful, but for Bud the pain will never pass.

Mike and Bud shared many common interests together; one of those interests was watching older movies. They were particularly fond of ones which had Robert DiNiro in the cast. When the warmer weather came around they both would be found aboard their favorite fishing vessel, the Captain Lou sailing out of Freeport harbor. Bud also shared his passion for the Doo-Wop music of the 50's and 60's with Mike, and he immediately became an avid fan as well. Mike's appreciation for this music would lead him to the frequent use of the expression "back in the day." As their closeness grew the usual roles of father and son soon were transformed into that of best friends and they were inseparable. They shared everything with each other; but their strongest commonality was their love for each other.

Not long after 9/11 Bud decided to undertake a special project in his backyard. He had constructed a huge shed which dwarfs his entire yard. What is unique about this project is that the project is an exact reproduction of Mike's firehouse in Prospect Heights drawn and constructed to scale. He has been able to capture and highlight every minuscule aspect of that firehouse. It is apparent that this was a well thought-out undertaking that required a great deal of patience and vision. Bud is a talented craftsman who has an attention to detail that rivals what is found on a Walt Disney production set. His workmanship bears credit to his remarkable talents. Bud had said that the project was a healthy diversion from his grief that he was experiencing soon after that horrific September day. When I witnessed Bud's project I couldn't help but sense that there was something else present within it too. As I viewed it I began to sense a strong spiritual connection manifesting itself between Mike and Bud emanating through this rather impressive presentation.

Losing her beloved son Michael has left Pat Kiefer heartbroken. Her eyes light up and she beams with pride as she fondly recalls the memories of her son. Throughout his life Michael had given Pat countless moments of joy that are forever etched in her heart. Pat loved his giant ever present smile. A relative of hers once said to "if you need something, pray to Michael to ask God for it; even God can't say no to that smile." Michael would always leave cards for Pat letting her know how much he loved her. On Saturday September 8, 2001 she found one such card on her kitchen table addressed to Mommy and Daddy. It was a beautiful card that bore the message of a son's love for his parents. When she had asked him why he sent it he simply relied "just because I love you." Sadly this was the last card that Pat and Bud would ever receive from Michael.

Pat wears a locket around her neck that carries a picture of her beloved Michael. Pat remembers that Mike would never pass her by without giving her a kiss. She recalls going to St. Mary's High School swim meets with Bud, and Mike would jump out of the pool to run over and kiss them both in front of a huge crowd. He was never intimidated by what others might have thought or felt; his love for his parents was unconditional. This love for his parents would have former New York City Mayor Rudy Guiliani, who spoke at his funeral, say through his tears, "I wish that my children were as thoughtful and caring as Michael."

Every Saturday evening if Mike wasn't working Pat and he would attend Mass at St. Catherine of Sienna. This was a very special time for Pat as she was able to witness her son maturing into a young man whose faith was deepening as well. Pat cherished that time she was able to spend with Michael. Mike readily acknowledged the important role that his parents had played in introducing him to his faith. Now, Pat was able to see the fruits that their efforts had reaped.

Pat remains truly amazed by the depth of Michael's faith; she had never witnessed someone that young with such ardent devotion. Attending Mass however isn't the same for Pat anymore; although she finds herself more engaged in prayer than before. Pat has struggled both logically and emotionally with Michael's death. She is no different than any other mother who has lost a child. From an intellectual perspective there is no sense that can be made of out the events of that day. No matter how hard one might try there remains no logical explanation for such an act of depraved indifference to human life. Her only reality is that she has lost her beloved son. Prayer offers some relief, but she sometimes finds herself in conflict with words such as "as we forgive those who trespass against us."

The loss of their Michael has placed a great deal of stress on all the Kiefer's, and Bud believes that stress can bring about other issues as well. They are grateful for the love and support of their daughters and their spouses. Pat and Bud are also blessed with two young grandsons Jack and Michael, and they both offer a world of sunshine into their lives. Another of the positive forces in their life has been the FDNY Counseling Unit and the help that they have received over the years. They both acknowledge the efforts of one counselor in particular, Gerry Moriarty. Gerry became a counselor after retiring as a Lieutenant with the FDNY, having spent more than twenty years with the Department.

Sadly losing Michael isn't the only tragedy to befall the Kiefer family. Their daughter Kerri was diagnosed with Multiple Sclerosis in 2008. Then when their daughter Lauren was five months pregnant with him; their grandson Jack was diagnosed with a very rare and often deadly congenital heart defect in which the left side of the heart does not develop. Jack would be born with half a heart. At the time, Lauren and her husband Rob refused the advice of their doctors to give up on the pregnancy. Instead, they brought him to New York- Presbyterian Morgan Stanley Children's Hospital. Jack went through a series of three very complex operations, the first of which was performed when he was just 4 days old. Each surgery carried significant risk of serious complications. However, Jack proved to be an incredibly resilient patient and the surgeries were enormously successful. His condition however still places him with the risk of him having to possibly become a candidate for a transplant.

For the present Jack is a healthy and very active young boy, and he has a smile that I sensed resembles the smile that was always on his Uncle Mike's face. In fact New York- Presbyterian Morgan Stanley Children's Hospital used Jack's photo in one of their ad campaigns. Jack's smiling face could be found in billboards, and on subways and buses throughout the New York City area. Alongside his photo is a quote from him "I had a broken heart. They fixed it and now I have a special heart."

Though they endured all these adversities the Kiefer family has survived. There is resilience that permeates from this family and it becomes obvious that the cement that holds them together is the love that they have for each other.

On July 18, 2002 the Kiefer family held a memorial service for Michael. The memorial was held at his parish St. Catherine of Sienna, and was well attended. Mike's body and those of all his comrades from Ladder 132 were never recovered. Pat and Bud recall meeting so many people at the memorial who they didn't know, but who knew Michael. Pat told me of five women in their seventies who came to the memorial as a group. After introducing themselves they explained that they swam every day at the town pool, the same pool that Mike was a lifeguard at. They told Pat that Mike greeted each of them with a hug and a kiss when they arrived at the pool. These ladies thought of Mike as their personal lifeguard, as he made their day every time they met him. Pat also met a local night watchman from the nearby Roosevelt Field Shopping Mall. The watchman recounted how Mike would arrive at the mall shortly before closing time at night. Mike was dressed in full firefighting clothes and carrying a length of firefighting hose. Mike would race up and down the stairs for hours on end preparing for the physical examination for the FDNY. Over the course of time he and the watchman developed a friendship, the watchman offering Mike encouragement as flew up and down the staircase.

The Kiefer's refuse to become victims for a second time; hence they remain vigilant in keeping Michael's sacrifice alive. They have donated a van to the FDNY Fire Family Transport Foundation. This van proudly bears the name of Firefighter Michael Kiefer on its windows. It is used to transport firefighters seriously injured in the line of duty and their families back and forth from hospital and doctors' appointments. Ironically many of these firefighters are suffering the lingering effects of their exposure to the atmosphere while they toiled at Ground Zero. The Kiefer family also raises funds for the New York City Firefighters Burn Center and Hope for Warriors. They proudly acknowledge the excellent work that these organizations routinely do and encourage others to support their efforts.

Each year since 9/11 the Kiefer family has organized and held a 5K race/walk on the Boardwalk in Long Beach, where Mike was a lifeguard. Funds from this event are given to charities in Michael's name. On the Boardwalk at Long Beach a memorial bench has been erected which acknowledges Mike's sacrifice and his service to the community. This bench also serves as the starting line for this commemorative race. There is a plaque attached to the bench which reminds everyone who sees it that Mike was both a Long Beach City Lifeguard and a New York City Firefighter. The plaque bears the following profound inscription that fittingly describes Mike and how he chose to live his life. "He Fulfilled His Calling, and Always Gave His Best."

In the fall of each year Bud organizes a Dinner Dance to raise funds for Michael's charities as well. The title of the event is called "Back in the Day with Mike." The theme of the evening's activities is a Doo Wopp music revival. This was the same music that both Mike and his father had come to enjoy. Bud arranges to have several of the top groups from the late fifties and early sixties on hand for a top rate performance. He also procures the services of a popular radio DJ from that genre too. This radio personality use his air time to help promote this noteworthy event. Along with the DJ and other volunteers Bud has been able to make this an event that quickly sells out every year. As with the other Kiefer fundraisers all the proceeds from this event also are donated to a charity in Mike's name too.

Mike Kiefer was only twenty-five years old when he reached his goal in life. Some people reach their goals much later in life, while others may never reach their goal. Mike's life was tragically cut short. His kind and gentle manner along with his great smile made him someone everyone wanted to be friends with. In his short life his kindness and gentleness allowed him to touch upon the lives of so many people in such a positive way. Mike will always be in the memories of those lives he touched, and he always remains etched in the heart and soul of Pat and Bud, and his sisters along with their spouses Rob and Anthony.

10

Firefighter Michael Cawley FDNY

MARGARET AND JACK CAWLEY

My sorrow is such that I feel a sword has pierced my heart.
—Margaret Cawley

Michael Cawley was the firstborn child of Jack and Margaret Cawley. After their marriage, Jack and Margaret settled in the Jackson Heights neighborhood of Queens. As the family began to grow, it soon became apparent that more living space was a necessity. So, three years after Michael's birth, the family purchased their first home in the Flushing section of Queens; they still reside there today. Their new home was only few hundred feet away from Mary's Nativity—Saint Ann. The church would serve as a focal point in Michael's early years. He would receive his elementary schooling there and proudly serve as an altar server. Mary's Nativity was also the parish where the family members would worship, and the Cawley children received the Sacraments there. It would also become the parish where Michael's memorial Mass, and later his funeral Mass, would be celebrated.

Michael's family was not much different from the other families in the neighborhood. The typical blue-collar area of

New York City is dotted with one- and two-family homes on relatively small parcels of land. Parks and ball fields provide an excellent milieu to raise children in a safe environment. Middle-income families, many with both parents working, represent the framework of the community. Like most New York City neighborhoods, the population is a melting pot. It is representative of all races, creeds, and nationalities, offering all—both young and old—the opportunity to develop relationships with neighbors from around the world. The neighborhood is best defined by the hardworking people who pay attention to their children, obey the law, pay their taxes, vote, and go to church.

Margaret Cawley asked me an unanswerable question: "Why? How could someone be consumed with that much hate to kill so many innocent people?" As I thought about her question, something resonated within me. What struck me was her concern for her son and for the other people who were murdered on that tragic day. Her pain is personal, yet there is also a genuine concern for others. She knows the grief that this event has brought, and she feels for those who share that same sorrow. Margaret is an extremely compassionate woman. It is a virtue that permeates through her, and it becomes obvious to anyone she encounters.

Compassion and empathy are required tools in Margaret's profession. She is a registered nurse, but something else also becomes apparent when talking with Margaret. She is an extremely intelligent and educated woman. She is filled with life and fueled with an energy that compels her to be the best she can be. Besides having attained an RN and a BSN, Margaret proudly holds several postgraduate degrees. She went on to become a licensed nurse practitioner with a specialty in oncology. One key component of her practice in oncology is that Margaret serves as a grief counselor for patients and their families. Margaret Cawley is no stranger to death and the sorrow that accompanies it.

***

It is seven o'clock in the morning on September 12, 2001, and Margaret Cawley's living room is filled with firefighters. The firefighters are Michael's friends and coworkers; a somber numbness begins to fill the room. She and Jack have been informed that their son has been confirmed as one of the unaccounted for by the New York City Fire Department. This is a scene that is occurring in the 342 other homes of New York City firefighters who live in and around the metropolitan area that morning. It is also a scenario that is occurring in nearly three thousand other homes across the United States and around the world.

The Cawley family is overcome with sorrow and grief. Their world has been turned upside down. Their concerns and prayers are focused on finding Michael; they are not alone. The nation and the world are joined together in prayer and in the hope that some great miracle might take place. The world has slowed down, and people are reflective. There is a heightened awareness of those around us, and we are reminded of our own mortality. The media provided the world frightening images of planes crashing into the towers and their eventual collapse. Those cameras shared a daily record of hundreds of firefighters, police officers, and construction workers unraveling tons of twisted steel in the hopes of finding someone.

Margaret is thrust into a strange new world, dealing with people she never thought she would have any contact with. The Cawley's once-serene lifestyle is suddenly usurped from them. The media and others make their presence known, causing an air of apprehension that leaves the family in a state of unease. Numerous agencies representing federal, state, and local governments reach out to the Cawley's and the families of the victims to offer their services. Though well intentioned, many are accompanied with the traditional bureaucratic red tape that is often associated with government agencies. For Margaret, this places another layer of stress on her and adds to the surrealism of the entire state of affairs. She is interviewed by FBI agents who declare Michael's death a homicide.

Not certain if Michael will ever be recovered, the family holds a memorial service on October 6, 2001. Memorial services were commonplace in the aftermath of September 11, 2001. New York City Fire Department line-of-duty funerals are usually attended by the department and local dignitaries. The events associated with 9/11 were anything but usual. In the weeks and months after the attack on the World Trade Center, all the FDNY funerals and memorials were attended by firefighters, local dignitaries, and elected officials. The elected officials attending these funeral were representative of city, state, and federal governments. The representatives had been sent to offer condolences and address the families of the firefighters. Having additional speakers address those assembled increased the length of time for these funerals and memorial services. The average time for these ceremonies was nearly four hours. There was also a significant media presence at the services—both print and electronic.

**

On the morning of Michael's memorial, Margaret is overwhelmed by the turnout from the department, but she is also puzzled by the presence of so many people she doesn't know. Strangers and the media at Michael's service are very unnerving for Margaret. One public official will address those assembled and offer the government's assurance that justice will be served. He states that our planes are on bombing missions, avenging that horrific event. A very private and personal ceremony is beginning to take on a different shape than what the Cawley's had originally planned.

A month later, the Cawley family receives the bittersweet

news that Michael has been recovered. The family is greatly relieved that they have Michael back—and he can finally be laid to rest. However; it reopens wounds that hadn't even begun to heal, adding to an already traumatic situation. The Cawley family begins to make arrangements for a wake and funeral Mass. Ever mindful of the unwanted notoriety that befell Michael's memorial; Margaret and Jack make every effort to see that the funeral is a much more private ceremony. After the funeral, Michael is laid to rest at Mount Saint Mary's Cemetery—a little more than a mile from his childhood home.

Professional caregivers agree that men and women mourn a loss differently. Jack Cawley would find himself leaning on his faith to give him comfort after the loss of Michael. Jack was raised in what many today would call a traditional Catholic home. He was sure that Michael had gone on to his reward in heaven, yet human nature is such that we are always in need of some form of proof or verification.

Several months after Michael's funeral, Jack would have a chance encounter with one of the FDNY's Catholic chaplains. This chaplain was also at the World Trade Center on the morning of September 11, 2001. During their conversation the priest had mentioned that prior to the collapse of the buildings he had administered the Sacrament of the Sick to all those present. The Catholic Church teaches that this sacrament helps unite those who are suffering with Jesus' saving and healing power. Through this sacrament people receive forgiveness for their sins and comfort in their suffering; they are restored in spirit; and sometimes they even experience the return of physical health. Hearing that Michael had received the Sacrament of the Sick prior to his death, Jack's faith assured him that his son had received his reward in heaven. For Jack this news greatly helped in relieving some of the stress that he had been under.

***

Not long after Michael's funeral, Margaret went back to work at Booth Memorial Hospital. She explained her return to work saying; she was there physically, but emotionally she was thousands of miles away. She struggles deeply with the loss of Michael; she misses him dearly and wishes he were there. Around her neck, she wears a locket that bears the picture of her beloved Michael. She is extremely sad and finds herself crying far too often. At work, she is grateful that she has her own office since it offers her a safe sanctuary for a few moments during the workday so she can collect her composure. She finds herself crying a good deal at home as well. As a trained grief counselor, Margaret is aware that she needs to talk to someone.

Margaret reaches out to a counselor who is well trained in this field for guidance. After two visits, the counselor tells Margaret that it might take four to six years to begin to feel better. Margaret understands this as well as her advisor does; healing takes time, and it is also a personal journey. She knows that the journey won't be a straight path. It will be filled with twists and turns and lined with bumps. Margaret knows that she must take this journey alone. She is aware that her faith, though already tested, will be a vital component in her journey. Margaret is grateful that she has been blessed with a deep faith.

In the days following 9/11, the New York City Fire Department's medical bureau and counseling services are inundated with requests for assistance from members and family members of those lost on that tragic date. The effects of the tragedy are just beginning to reverberate throughout the department's family. The department's medical officers realize the depths of the issues, and they respond to the requests immediately and in the most caring and professional manner. These are unchartered waters for the department and the caregivers. The counseling services unit adopts methods and systems to best care for the diverse needs of all who require assistance. One such system is creating a group that is entirely composed of just the parents of those firefighters who were lost at the World Trade Center.

Margaret Cawley sees this parents' group as an opportunity to help ease some of her sorrow, and she eagerly decides to join. The group consists of a few dozen parents who had lost firefighter sons at the World Trade Center. The group is led by counselors from the FDNY's counseling services, and they meet weekly. None of the parents know each other, but their common bond makes the group comfortable. Margaret greatly values the group and the benefits of companionship and comfort from sharing each other's stories. Over the course of their time together, the parents will forge lasting friendships. Members who feel overwhelmed might reach out to other group members. A simple phone call to another member brings a great deal of comfort.

∗∗

"Mayday ... Mayday ... firefighter trapped." Those are the words that no firefighter ever wants to hear. Sadly that message was transmitted early on Sunday morning, January 23, 2005, for a fire in a tenement building on East 178th Street in the Bronx. It was a cold morning, and the city had experienced a sixteen-inch snowfall the previous night. What was unknown to the firefighters was that the building had undergone numerous illegal alterations that were not visible upon their arrival. These alterations subdivided the existing apartments into various illegal single-room occupancies that endangered firefighters and placed the innocent tenants who resided there at grave risk too.

Because of these illegal alterations, a vital means of egress was blocked for six firefighters on the fourth floor. The firefighters were searching for victims and any extension of the fire. Without any warning, the conditions on the fourth floor deteriorated, and the firefighters' position on the floor became untenable. The six were forced to leap out of the fourth-floor windows to escape the intense fire. Two of the firefighters would make the ultimate sacrifice. Lieutenant John G. Bellew and Lieutenant Curtis Meyran succumbed to their injuries that day. The four other firefighters were transported to area hospitals; three were in critical condition, and one was in serious condition. Tragically, several hours later, Firefighter Richard Sclafani would also make the supreme sacrifice in another fire in Brooklyn. That day would come to be remembered in the New York City Fire Department as Black Sunday.

***

On bitter cold Sunday afternoon, Jack and Margaret Cawley enter Saint Barnabas Hospital in the Bronx. Their younger son, Brendan, is one of the six firefighters who were forced to leap from that Bronx building fire. As a probationary firefighter, Brendan had graduated from the fire academy less than a month earlier. Margaret feels some relief that she was able to speak with Brendan prior to their arrival at the hospital. As a registered nurse, she knows that she needs to speak to the doctors and other caregivers. Not even four years have passed since Michael had made the supreme sacrifice; now Margaret finds herself pleading with the doctors to save her younger son's life.

Brendan had landed on his back, shattering his right shoulder, cracking his ribs, splitting his skull, and collapsing a lung. He used his right arm to pull himself up to a sitting position so he could breathe easier and then he passed out. Brendan would require major surgery and extensive rehabilitation sessions. Brendan believes that his older brother was watching over him that Sunday morning, and he credits Michael with saving him. He also credits Michael and the other firefighters killed on 9/11 for providing him with motivation during his recovery.

Brendan was determined to return to full duty and return to work at his firehouse. His recovery was slow and painful, and it required a great deal of fortitude. Brendan thought that his mother would have misgivings about his desire to return to full duty. When that issue presented itself to Margaret, she replied, "Brendan, if this is going to bring a smile to your face again, then I'm behind you. I support you." Thirty-four months after being trapped in that fourth-floor apartment, Brendan Cawley proudly reported for duty at his firehouse. Before he had left for work, Margaret kissed him, hugged him, wished him luck, and cautioned him to be safe.

Margaret is grateful that her prayers for Brendan have been answered and that he is whole again. Prayer has been a constant companion for Margaret as she travels on her journey, and she finds solace in the serenity of peaceful reflection. On the first few Mother's Days after 9/11, Margaret would attend a silent Mother's Day weekend retreat at the Saint Ignatius Retreat House on Long Island. The retreat offered a soothing tranquility while providing her with a warm setting for her thoughts and prayers. During the retreat, there were some open discussions, but the remaining hours were silent. After attending Mass on Mother's Day, Margaret would go home and prepare the foods that Kristin and Brendan liked. That custom would keep her busy, and the day would pass easier for her.

It is a daily routine for Jack and Margaret to visit Michael's grave. After more than a dozen years, they still miss Michael dearly. In the weeks and months after 9/11, a common mantra was heard all around the country: "Never forget." This slogan meant different things for different people. For Jack and Margaret, the words have a deep and well-defined meaning. The mantra became the driving force that propelled them into sharing Michael's life with the world. They are extremely proactive in keeping their son's memory alive. Jack and Margaret eagerly share their son's life story, and they emphasize all the lives that Michael was able to touch upon in such a short time. They have become tireless workers in Michael's foundation, dedicating their time and efforts to helping others in Michael's name. They have been blessed to remain connected with so many of Michael's friends from high school, college, and the fire department. These friends have stood shoulder to shoulder with the Cawley's, helping them spread the message of this fine young man's short life.

The Cawley's have an ongoing scholarship program in Michael's name for four students at the prestigious Archbishop Molloy Catholic High School in Queens. It is the same high school that Michael attended. Margaret recalls how much of a positive affect Molloy had on Michael during the four years that he attended the school. Margaret warmly remembers how Molloy provided Michael with the academic tools to advance and opened his eyes to the world around him. During his time at Molloy, Michael had the good fortune to make many friends. Margaret and Jack both agree that his time at Molloy fostered his maturity and, made him more cognizant of the world around him.

Molloy showed Michael many of the social justice issues of the day and exposed him to young people with special needs. At Molloy, Michael learned that he needed to become an agent of justice and service, standing alongside those who are marginalized by society. Molloy students are taught to recognize that they are lovingly created by God with unique gifts and talents which, through baptism, they are called to develop and share with the church and the community. Archbishop Molloy's school motto comes from the Roman Stoic philosopher Seneca: "Non scholae sed vitae." Translated it means not for school but for life. Surely, when one reflects on Michael's life, it becomes apparent that he is a perfect role model for today's young students at Molloy. Michael embodied the very ethos he learned at Molloy. Michael truly was a faithful son of Archbishop Molloy High School, and he is a son who all who have attended Molloy can take a great deal of pride in.

Jack, Margaret, and Michael's friends raise funds for a

summer camp in upstate New York. This camp is administered by the Marist Brothers, the same order of Brothers who teach at Molloy. This camp is designed to accommodate young people with special needs. Michael spent parts of his four summers at Molloy volunteering to this noteworthy cause. The Cawley family takes a great deal of pride in the camp, knowing how much it meant to Michael and how instrumental it was in his love of life.

A dear friend of Michael once summed up Michael by saying, "To him, it wasn't the years in his life but the life in his years."

A good deal of time has passed since 9/11, and Margaret still misses Michael dearly. Thinking about Margaret's journey, I'm reminded of the words from Saint Augustine in The Confessions: "Thou hast made us for thyself, Oh Lord, and our heart is restless until it finds its rest in thee." Surely Margaret's pierced heart rests with thee Oh Lord.

11

Captain Tommy Haskell FDNY

*A true leader has the confidence to stand alone, the
courage to make tough decisions, and the compassion
to listen to the needs of others. He does not set out
to be a leader, but becomes one by the equality
of his actions and the integrity of his intent.*
—Douglas MacArthur

Maureen and Tom Haskell settled in the Long Island community of Seaford. Tom was a New York City firefighter, and soon after they moved into their home, their first child, Tommy, made his arrival. Seaford is a small, close-knit suburban hamlet that is right on the bay across from Jones Beach. Seaford is a also a stone's throw away from some of Long Island's other more noted beaches, such as Gilgo, Long Beach, and Point Lookout. Growing up in such close proximity to the water afforded a young boy to experience swimming, surfing, and volleyball on a daily basis. Tommy would grow to love the beach, and Long Island provided him with the ideal playground.

Tommy was born with a true competitive nature, and from an early age, it was readily discernible that he possessed a natural flair for leadership. In Boy Scouts, Tommy would eagerly participate in honing his skills and abilities through the process of earning merit badges. In one such event, Tommy set a new record in his quest for a merit badge by swimming a one-mile race. Tommy's competiveness would eventually lead him to the football field. Football was the sport best suited for Tommy's skills. On the field, he was able to harness his natural athletic talents with his mental skills. The gridiron also gave Tommy the ideal backdrop to develop and hone his leadership qualities. Tommy would serve as a captain of his team in the junior division and in junior and senior high school. Tommy would eventually bring those assets to the New York City Fire Department's football team.

Tommy quickly learned that the skills he developed on the field were gifts, and as such, he should share them with others. After he moved up from midget football, he returned to help coach. He did the same thing in baseball, offering his services as an umpire for Little League games. When it came time to step down from playing football for the fire department, Tommy stepped up and helped coach there as well. This virtue of sharing and returning knowledge and skills that he acquired were attributes that would always make Tommy Haskell stand out from others. His demeanor would quickly give rise to him earning the respect of his fellow firefighters and his bosses.

Tommy was called to the New York City Fire Department just as he was about to enter his senior year at Saint John's University. Determined not to be denied what he had spent three years working toward, he transferred to night school. That enabled him the opportunity to finish his degree and graduate on schedule from Saint John's. Each evening after he had spent a full day at the FDNY fire academy's probationary firefighter school, Tommy headed off to Saint John's University. Whenever Tommy had some spare time, he started studying for the lieutenant's test—even though his probationary status prevented him from taking the test. That was just one of many indications of how driven Tommy Haskell was, and that drive would eventually propel him up the ranks at breakneck speed.

Family and friends recall how Tommy would often disappear at parties or other social gatherings. Tommy would drift off to the garage or some other remote area of the house to study for an upcoming promotional examination. Promotional examinations in the FDNY are based on civil service examinations. They are scheduled every four years and are extremely competitive; therefore, attaining a high score on the tests is imperative. Tommy Haskell was aware of the competitiveness of the examinations, and he was steadfastly determined to do the very best that he could on them.

In 1993, Tommy's two younger brothers, Timmy and Ken, were sworn in to the FDNY. What had made that event even more special was that Tommy's brother-in-law, Kevin, and his cousin Frankie were also appointed in that class. Maureen Haskell recalls how proud Tommy was that day: "You would have thought he was the parent." He cherished the opportunity to share his lifelong passion with his family. When Tommy's father passed away, it was a natural transition to assume the role of paternal leadership. Caring for people came rather easily to Tommy. Caring for family was an innate quality that he possessed; it defined him as a person.

Seaford offered many athletic opportunities for Tommy, and it provided him with the milieu to make friends. Tommy would cherish these friends, and they would forever remain an intrinsic part of his life. Here he would meet the love of his life, his partner: Barbara. When Tommy and Barbara were married, it seemed to be a natural progression. They had been high school sweethearts at Seaford High School. They were blessed to have three beautiful daughters: Meaghan, Erin, and Tara. Tommy would have a new destination on the weekends. He soon became a regular at the soccer fields to cheer on his daughters in their matches. Tommy brought that same determination that he displayed on the football field into making a loving home for Barbara and the girls.

Even before they had children, Barbara and Tommy would

visit Disneyworld almost every year. Disneyworld is the world's most preeminent family theme park, and as such, it is equally famous for its long lines. This was just another challenge for Tommy to master; he enjoyed making issues non-issues. He would draw up a precise strategy so that he and his family could visit more sights and rides than most other people. His attention to detail at home with his family and in the firehouse showed an intricate building block in his leadership quality.

Tommy's house always had an American flag proudly on display. As the oldest son of a former United States Marine, he knew only too well what that banner represented—and the price that many had paid for it to wave. Tommy and Barbara's house also had another tradition: Christmas. Christmas at the Haskell house was a very special and fun-filled time of the year. After Thanksgiving, Tommy would take two weeks off to set up his phenomenal Christmas village. The village was no small undertaking; it required him to work from 7:00 a.m. to 10:00 p.m. every day before it was completed. He named the village Barbara's Gardens, Meaghanville, Erinburgh, and Taratown after the women in his life. He would always have a house lighting ceremony, and he incorporated a question-and-answer segment for the different scenes in the village. The first child who could answer the questions correctly received a chocolate kiss from Tommy's train as it traveled around and through his village.

One of the primary requirements of working in the New York City Fire Department is the ability to learn to work as a member of a team. Teamwork has always been an essential component in the fire service. Every team needs a leader for a leader to be effective, and in the world of firefighting, a leader must inspire and influence others through character and example. Tommy was respected and admired by the firefighters under his command. Tommy's superiors also recognized his talents and referred to him as "The Whiz Kid." His rapid ascent up the ranks coupled with his natural leadership abilities deservedly earned him the respect and admiration of his bosses.

Tommy Haskell lived his life adhering to the three Fs: family, fire department, and football.

FIREFIGHTER TIMMY HASKELL FDNY

If you have men who will exclude any of God's creatures from the shelter of compassion and pity, you will have men who will deal likewise with their fellow men.
— Saint Francis of Assisi

When Timmy Haskell was two years old, his mother would say, "White."

Timmy would respond, "Black."

As a small child, Timmy would always challenge Maureen, but by the time he had reached four years old, he was her strongest ally. To say that Timmy was an active child would be a serious understatement. Mischief and a desire to challenge the unknown were the fuels that sparked Timmy's early development. His enthusiastic lifestyle would soon have Tom and Maureen spending a considerable amount of time in the emergency room. Broken bones and sutures were everyday events in the Haskell home when Timmy was a child. That daredevil approach toward life only increased as he matured into manhood.

As a child, Timmy could always be found on a skateboard or his dirt bike. The faster he went, the bigger the thrill he received. Growing up in the seaside community of Seaford, Timmy was blessed to have the bay right outside his back door. The water became a playground for Timmy to satisfy his adventurous yearnings. Maureen fondly recalls how Timmy developed a relationship with the police officers who regularly patrolled their neighborhood. Whenever a complaint for someone racing a dirt bike recklessly was received, they didn't have to look very hard for the culprit. As Timmy matured, his childhood toys would be replaced by speedboats and motorcycles. Scuba diving became another passion as he grew older.

Timmy always had an insatiable drive to experience new and daring thrills; it was an important part of his personality. Shortly before 9/11, Timmy had been actively engaged in learning to fly planes, and he was well on his way to getting his pilot's license. Timmy's dad had earned his pilot's license while he was in the United States Marine Corps. Maureen sees many similarities between Tom and Timmy. They both enjoyed being the life of the party, and each was filled with an unquenchable desire for adventure.

One aspect about the fire department that Timmy appreciated was the advantage that the work schedule provides. This flexible schedule allowed him the time to purse his passion for adventure. During the summer, Timmy could be found scuba diving, jet-skiing, or waterskiing. The winter months offered him opportunities to bring that same enthusiasm to the snow-covered mountains. When Timmy wasn't working, it was a sure thing that he was off on some undertaking that somehow incorporated a certain amount of risk-taking.

Maureen recalls Timmy as having a natural entrepreneurial talent as a youngster. After mastering three paper routes, Timmy was able to secure employment in a delicatessen. Working in the delicatessen, in such a close-knit community, provided him with the framework to establish relationships with every family in the neighborhood. It was understood by all in his community; that whenever a problem arose, it was Timmy who you could always rely on to offer assistance.

It was quite common to find Timmy helping a neighbor with an automotive or mechanical problem. If he wasn't at the deli, he was wearing his tool belt with his sleeves rolled up, deeply engrossed in some repair project. Timmy enjoyed interacting with his neighbors, and his neighbors appreciated his assistance. They also enjoyed spending the time with him. Timmy's openness and friendly manner made him beloved in the community.

When the fire department decided to create squad companies, they wanted to staff them with elite members of the department. In addition to responding to fires, the squad companies would be required to respond to various emergencies throughout the city. Special responses could range from hazardous material response to train derailments or an airplane crash. The process of being selected to one of these units was extremely competitive, and it required physical and mental assessments. Timmy Haskell saw this opportunity as the ideal combination to hone his firefighting skills and experience new and daring adventures. He immediately submitted his request to be assigned to a squad company and was accepted.

Timmy had been infatuated with tools since he was a child. He brought that infatuation along to the firehouse. He was so engrossed with tools that his fellow firefighters affectionately referred to him as "Gadget Man." Timmy had a propensity for bringing a new tool or gadget to the firehouse. He was always looking for something that could benefit his unit in a fire or an emergency. Timmy was the type of firefighter who was never off duty. His thoughts were always focused on the job, and he concentrated on how he could become a more proficient firefighter.

There was also a very different side of Timmy Haskell—a much different perspective than the daredevil persona he often showed. This side of Timmy was caring and compassionate. Timmy loved animals. As a child, he would tend to a stray dog or a sick bird. He was fascinated by animals and read as much as he could about them. His love of animals would endear him to all the pet owners in the community. Aware of his knowledge of animals, they would seek his advice on caring for their own pets.

Timmy's sister Dawn recalls an event that occurred a few months prior to September 11, 2001. Timmy was out for a ride on his bicycle when he stumbled upon a pigeon with the top part of its beak torn off. He took the bird home and nursed it back to health. For several months, he monitored the bird's progress daily until it was fully healed. Timmy used an eyedropper to deliver food to the injured animal. "He was always rescuing something," Dawn said.

Timmy would volunteer his time to instruct students at elementary schools during fire prevention week. Timmy and his Dalmatian performed demonstrations at schools near his firehouse. He was always accompanied by Blaze. Timmy developed a strong relationship with Blaze and taught him many skills. Timmy would say, "'Blaze, your clothes are on fire. What do you do?" Blaze would respond by dropping and rolling to Timmy's command. As expected, the young children were amazed by Blaze's performance. Timmy was able provide them with a vivid example of what to do if they found themselves in a similar situation.

Before Timmy entered the fire department, he was a deputy sheriff in Nassau County. His many friends from the sheriff's department would miss Timmy when he left for the fire department, but they knew that was where needed to be. Timmy loved life, and he loved to laugh. He loved to make those around him laugh as well—even at his own expense. He was the life of the party and took a great deal of pride in seeing others enjoy themselves. His natural concern for others both on a social and emotional level was one of his most desirable qualities.

Timmy Haskell's ability to connect with people on different levels made him someone who would endear himself to others. His genuine concern for others would ultimately manifest itself on that fateful morning of September 11, 2001. Timmy had just gotten off a fifteen-hour night tour at just about the same time the hijacked planes crashed into the World Trade Center. As he was walking toward the subway station, Timmy began to notice thick smoke billowing from the Twin Towers. Timmy dashed back to his firehouse, donned his firefighting gear, and sped off to the burning towers. It was his last response as a member of the New York City Fire Department.

MAUREEN HASKELL

And He will raise you up on eagle's wings,
Bear you on the breath of dawn,
Make you to shine like the sun,
And hold you in the palm of His Hand.
You need not fear the terror of the night,
Nor the arrow that flies by day,
Though thousands fall about you,
Near you it shall not come.

On the evening of September 11, 2001, the phone rang in the Haskell's Seaford home. Maureen Haskell could feel her heart thumping with each ring. She hesitantly picked up the receiver and said hello. On the other end of the line was a familiar voice; that of her son Ken.

Maureen had a mother's intuition that something was not right. She had been glued to the television all day just like everyone else in the country, and she felt that what she had feared most was about to become a horrible reality. She said, "Have you found out about your brothers?"

"No one's coming home, Mom," Ken replied.

The thought of losing one son at that tragic event is horrific; losing two sons on the same day at the same incident becomes unfathomable. Maureen Haskell's world came crashing down around her. No matter how scholarly one might be, there were no words that could be comforting to Maureen at that moment. Maureen has been endowed with a deep faith, but even the deepest faith would be challenged under such dire circumstances.

Maureen credits much of her faith formation to her father, a convert to Catholicism. The Catholic tradition teaches that every man is bound by the natural law to seek the true religion, embrace it when found, and conform his life to its principles and precepts. Often those who discover faith later in life develop a deeper understanding of it.

Maureen Haskell had spent most of her adult life working in the New York State court system. One might mistakenly conclude that working in an environment that places one amidst an assortment of nefarious people on a daily basis might make a person indifferent or apathetic. Nothing could be further from the truth in Maureen's case. She is a very private woman who has a great sense of humor and has been blessed with a genuine compassion for humankind. Maureen has a true zest for life, and she nurtured that trait in both Tommy and Timmy. Unfortunately, Maureen was faced with the difficult task of burying her two beloved sons.

Tommy Haskell's body would never be recovered from the World Trade Center. The Haskell family would arrange for a memorial service to be held in honor of Tommy. It was not unusual; in fact, many of the people lost that fateful day were never recovered. Several days after 9/11, the remains of Timmy Haskell were recovered. The Haskell family arranged a funeral Mass for him. Both the Haskell brothers' services were conducted with full FDNY honors and were attended by family, friends, and members of the department.

Being a very private person, Maureen would not allow herself to grieve in a public setting. She chose to grieve in solitude rather than in view of anyone. She felt it was important to remain strong for her children, grandchildren, and particularly her mother. She is very private, and she is a strong-willed and determined woman. Hundreds of friends came to pay their respects to the brothers.

During the funerals for her sons, Maureen was greatly

moved by the amount people who gathered to pay their respects to her family. Watching such a vast outpouring resonated with Maureen; she was able to witness how many people's lives her two beloved sons had touched in so many positive ways.

No long after Tommy and Timmy's funerals, Maureen recalls how she struggled both spiritually and intellectually, desperately searching to make some sense out of that horrific event. How could the evil people who perpetrated the tragedy believe that they would be rewarded with heaven? Surely they couldn't be with her sons. She couldn't grasp how this evil act was perceived by some as heavenly ordained. Searching for answers and a sense of direction, Maureen found herself attending daily Mass at Saint William the Abbott. Maureen believed that her parish would offer her a comforting sanctuary where she could be alone with her thoughts and prayers. Saint William's did offer her that sanctuary, but when she looked into the daily Mass intentions book one morning and saw Tommy and Timmy's names, she knew it was time to talk to someone.

Maureen was friendly with one of the parish priests at Saint William's, and she reached out to Father Steve. He had been a constant companion to the Haskell family in the days following 9/11 and knew firsthand the dynamics facing the Haskell family. Father Steve assured Maureen that it was all right to be angry—and that she had every right to feel that way. He added that praying for her sons helped keep them alive. Maureen views herself as having two options at that moment in her life. She could live her life as a victim or stand tall and serve as an example of someone who couldn't be beaten down. She chose the latter.

Maureen returned to work shortly after the funerals, but she felt unease upon her return. Her coworkers were all greatly concerned for her and expressed their desire to help her in any way possible. A sense of disconnect and a feeling of melancholy left Maureen extremely sad. There were times at work when she would break down in tears. Maureen felt alone, particularly without her husband. Maureen realized that the events occurring in her life were unique, and she needed to be with people who could understand the grief she was enduring.

When the fire department's counseling unit started its parents' group, Maureen decided to join. Like most of the other parents, there was some initial trepidation, but it rapidly disappeared soon after the group began. Everyone became comfortable with each other. Maureen is grateful for the compassion and companionship that the group offered its members. By sharing their common grief and problems with one another, the group was a fundamental tool in the healing process. The group also afforded Maureen a network of new friends. Maureen and her friends have remained in close contact both socially and in a supportive manner.

One day after attending a parents' group meeting, Maureen met a firefighter who was working at the World Trade Center on the morning of September 11. He spoke to her about the chance encounter he had with Timmy that fateful day. As the firefighter was entering the tower, he noticed Timmy leaving the building with an injured civilian in his arms. Once he was outside the building, Timmy passed the injured person to the paramedics. Having completed this task, Timmy Haskell reentered the tower—never to be seen alive again. For some people, it might be difficult to understand why Timmy didn't stay with that person rather than reentering the building and exposing himself to more danger. Maureen Haskell knows that all her children would rise to any occasion whenever it presented itself. Hearing the details of Timmy's unselfishness in the face of extreme adversity fills Maureen with great pride.

In the months and years after September 11, Maureen Haskell has been forced to face a multitude of severe challenges. One of her grandchildren, Ryan, was born with serious medical problems. This problem would require more than a dozen major operations. The operations were occurring at a rate of almost one per year. Though he hasn't had any more operations, Ryan still faces many lingering medical issues.

In 2011, Long Island was hit hard by Hurricane Irene. Maureen's house was on the shoreline and did not escape the ravages of Irene. Although her family had helped her prepare for the storm, its effects were devastating. Maureen's house would suffer serious water damage from the flooding that accompanied Irene. Maureen would lose a significant amount of the contents in her home. The items included many mementos from her children and grandchildren. Losing the last pieces of her memories with Tommy and Timmy was extremely difficult, and Maureen admits it set back her healing. Gone were pictures from their youth and the usual sentimental items of their children that parents relish. Hurricane Irene would leave Maureen without her home for more than four months. Maureen is ever so grateful for the generosity of her daughter and son-in-law during that period. Dawn and Mario provided Maureen with a place to stay by welcoming her into their home for four months.

In 2012, Maureen developed cancer for the second time. The cancer required major surgery, which was successful. The cancer is now in remission, and Maureen is grateful for the positive results that her doctors have reported. Maureen has faced this challenge in the same head-on manner that she has faced all of life's challenges. Maureen Haskell has a deep faith and is a very courageous woman.

After her surgery, Maureen returned home to continue her recuperation and to begin her recovery process. Five weeks after she returned home, Hurricane Sandy ravaged Long Island. It was unlike any hurricane in the past. The storm took all of Maureen's remaining possessions. The damage was devastating and left Maureen heartbroken. Refusing to surrender to the troubles that had fallen on her, Maureen made the necessary arrangements to have her house rebuilt. Once again, Dawn and Mario offered their home to Maureen. Maureen's house was rebuilt, and she returned home, but that was not without a host of issues.

More than two years removed from the storm, Maureen finds herself in a daily battle. She is not unlike any of the tens of thousands of other homeowners who Sandy had wreaked havoc upon. The daily routines of trying to unravel an immeasurable amount of red tape are beginning to take a toll on Maureen. She realizes that she is not the only person who was affected by Sandy, but this bureaucratic labyrinth is adding more stress to an already stressful situation. Many people who were affected by Sandy complain about a breakdown in the lines of communication, and that breakdown simply adds more frustration.

Maureen has lost all the mementos of a family's lifetime. She also lost what Tom and she had struggled for: a home filled with the memories of a lifetime. Maureen is steadfast in her praise and admiration for the assistance and support that her children, her daughters-in-law, and her son-in-law have provided during this trying ordeal. Without the support of her family, she doesn't know what she would have done.

The extremely difficult challenges that have befallen Maureen mirror the challenges that confronted Job. Scripture reveals the story of a holy man named Job who—with God's approval—is tried by Satan with severe afflictions to test his virtue. Job tolerates six great temptations with valiant patience—without any mention against God or waning in his faithfulness to God. This story extols the benefits of patience while offering solace and succor to those suffering. Maureen Haskell never complains and remains a faith-filled believer in God. Her patience and faith are virtues to be admired, and we all should aspire to possess them.

In the months after 9/11, the Seaford community would ban together and ensure that the events of that day would never be forgotten by its citizens. The community would erect a permanent monument on the high school campus to honor its graduates who perished at the World Trade Center. Besides the Haskell brothers, three other alums were killed that day. The community and the school district created the Patriot's Award. The award is administered by a committee of local residents; each year, five graduating seniors from Seaford High School are selected for this prestigious recognition. The Haskell family is very active in promoting this special award; it is only fitting since Seaford High School was a centerpiece in Tommy and Timmy's earlier years. Dawn and Ken serve as board members.

The 9/11 Patriot Award Committee invites students to serve the Seaford community and the country to make a difference. Students are encouraged to voluntarily perform at least one service activity during the school term. Their service pledge will be recognized at the annual candle-lighting ceremony on Patriot Day. The primary goal of the committee is inspire everyone to carry forward every day in their lives, through their actions toward others, the remarkable spirit of unity, understanding, and service that brought America and the world together in the aftermath of the September 11 attacks.

Not long after 9/11, Maureen Haskell donated a sum of money to the New York City Fire Department. These monies were earmarked for the department to purchase a new van for the Family Transport Foundation. The central focus of the foundation is assisting the families of firefighters in their times of greatest need to transport firefighters, family members, and department personnel to and from medical institutions and for care and family support. The van bears a customized logo of the Haskell brothers and a reminder of their sacrifice. Maureen is saddened that this van has amassed an enormous amount of mileage over the past few years. That large amount of mileage can be sadly attributed to 9/11. In the past few years, far too many firefighters have been diagnosed with an array of different cancers. Others battle pulmonary diseases. The van—and others like it—take active and retired firefighters to clinics and doctor appointments throughout the New York metropolitan area.

Maureen was not satisfied just having the van as a remembrance of Tommy and Timmy. A coworker, Steve Mendelsohn, suggested that she look into organizing a golf outing to help raise funds for the different charities. Steve explained the rudimentary procedures required to organize a golf outing to the Haskell family. Maureen and Ken created the Haskell Brothers Golf Outing at the Lido Beach Golf Club. Dawn is the tireless behind-the-scenes worker and helps make the event a yearly success. This outing has become a yearly event that is always filled to capacity. The participants in the outing represent a broad spectrum. Judges and prominent attorneys from the courts where Maureen worked, firefighters who worked with the Haskell brothers, childhood friends, neighbors, local dignitaries, and strangers all come together for this fun-filled event that raises significant funds for numerous charities. This outing contributes greatly in perpetuating the memory of the sacrifice of the Haskell brothers.

The FDNY Family Transport Foundation was one of the charities that has benefitted from this outing. The outing has also donated to the special needs group Angela's House in honor of Maureen's grandson, Ryan. The Haskell's have also responded to a support group for firefighters with cancer. The Haskell Brothers Golf Outing has afforded the Haskell family the opportunity to continue to contribute toward many worthwhile causes.

Over the last few years, the Haskell's have honored Hope for Wounded Warriors Project, and they have invited many of the heroes to participate in the outing. The outing is always the Thursday before Memorial Day and is always at Lido Beach, which is next door to Jones Beach. Every Memorial Day, the United States Navy's Blue Angels perform an airshow over Jones Beach. The Blue Angels represent the finest United States Navy and Marine Corps aviators, and they perform airshows that mesmerize crowds around the world.

On the Thursday before Memorial Day, the Blue Angels

practice their delicate maneuvers at breakneck speeds high over the oceanfront of Long Island's south shore. Maureen is amazed at how quiet and still the golf course becomes as the jets thunder overhead. Seeing the jets roar above brings back fond memories for Maureen of Tom and Timmy—and the passion for flying they both shared. Looking out on the golf course, the effect of the Blue Angels becomes quite evident as all the Wounded Warriors come to attention. Their chests fill with pride. It is noteworthy to observe the proud aura that comes over all the other golfers who are assembled for the special event. It is a memorable backdrop for an outing that honors two of our country's best.

The Haskell brothers may have been small-town kids, but their bravery has touched the hearts of a nation.

EPILOGUE

Interviewing the parents of firefighters has been an enlightening and inspiring experience. These parents will always share a common grief that the entire world also witnessed unfolding before them in the media. The effects of this tragic and horrific event will remain etched forever in their hearts and souls. During this process, I have gained a powerful insight from all the parents of these valiant firefighters; as a group, they have had to face a parent's worst nightmare. One dominant and shared attribute among all the families is the ability to confront loss with grace and dignity—even though, at times, they were encroached upon by the media and others. They all endured, having the privacy of their grief being compromised. As each anniversary presents itself, they are forced to deal with those encroachments all over again.

Through listening to their stories, I was granted the opportunity to become more enlightened by the depth of—and the many different characteristics of—grief. I have been equally inspired by the absolute resolve that all these parents have in perpetuating their sons' memories and sacrifices. All of the firefighters highlighted in the text shared a multitude of common virtues, but as the parents reflect on their sons' lives, their shared compassion for humanity comes to the forefront and unites them forever. That shared compassion for humanity was exemplified through their final act of courage. The common virtues found in each of these firefighters can readily be traced back to the parents instilling values in their sons and serving as ideal role models for them.

In the weeks following September 11, 2001, the families of all the firefighters who perished that day were overcome with stress and grief. Witnessing their sons' deaths on television—and then not knowing if they would ever be recovered—was far too much to endure. All of the parents strongly acknowledge the efforts and consideration that the FDNY's counseling services unit afforded them, particularly the care and concern of Gerry Moriarty and Trudy Hasnas. Both of these dedicated practitioners acknowledge the assistance and guidance they received from Dr. Diane Kane and Malachy Corrigan, who were instrumental in the forming of the family group.

In the dark days after September 11, 2001, it became apparent to those professional caregivers from the FDNY's counseling unit that they needed to employ new and different approaches in order to assist the members of the department and their families. The counselors readily admit that there was no boilerplate or schematic to draw from. The department and the counselors faced a staggering amount of members and family members who were desperately in need of help.

In the department's darkest hours, the FDNY's counseling unit rose to the task before them. Their concern and empathy for all the members and family members was a beacon that resonated throughout the department. The FDNY's medical officers played a major role in ensuring that all who were affected by the tragedy were cared for. No one was ever denied assistance, and every effort was exerted to help anyone who asked for help. All those caregivers brought compassion and empathy to all those in need, and all their efforts should never be forgotten.

Within the New York City Fire Department, there exists a special culture that isn't found in many other workplaces. It is a culture in which the families of the members are incorporated into the traditions of the department. While in probationary firefighter school at the fire academy, the families of the probationary firefighters are invited to a family day at the school. Parents, spouses, children, and other family members are given an opportunity to get better insights into the world of firefighting. The day's activities include classroom demonstrations and the chance to examine many of the department's resources. Later in the day, the probationary firefighters demonstrate their newly learned skills. This is done by creating a simulated fire in which the probationary firefighters demonstrate those skills through a live demonstration of the extinguishment of that fire.

Upon completion of their training, the department has a graduation ceremony for the probationary firefighters. Family members of the new firefighters are invited to attend the event, and it is always a standing-room-only crowd. In the aftermath of September 11, 2001, the FDNY's medical officers and the practitioners with the FDNY's counseling services were aware of the relationship that existed between the families of firefighters and the department. Cognizant of this fact, the medical officers took every step possible to ensure that the practitioners were knowledgeable in the dynamics of the department.

Made in the USA
Columbia, SC
26 September 2020